FREIRE
AND EDUCATION

One of the most influential educational philosophers of our times, Paulo Freire, contributed to a revolutionary understanding of education as an empowering and democratizing force in the lives of the disenfranchised. In this deeply personal introduction to the man and his ideas, Antonia Darder reflects on how Freire's work has illuminated her own life practices and thinking as an educator and activist. Including both personal memories and a never-before published, powerful dialogue with Freire himself, Darder offers a unique "analysis of solidarity," in mind and spirit. A heartfelt look at the ways Freire can still inspire a critically intellectual and socially democratic life, this book is certain to open up his theories in entirely new ways, both to those already familiar with his work and those coming to him for the first time.

Antonia Darder is Professor Emerita of Educational Policy, Organization, and Leadership at the University of Illinois at Urbana-Champaign and holds the Leavey Presidential Endowed Chair in Ethics and Moral Leadership in the School of Education at Loyola Marymount University.

D0140042

Routledge Key Ideas in Education Series

Series Editors: Greg Dimitriadis and Bob Lingard

Freud and Education, Deborah P. Britzman
Marx and Education, Jean Anyon
Foucault, Power, and Education, Stephen J. Ball
L.S. Vygotsky and Education, Luis C. Moll

FREIRE

AND EDUCATION

ANTONIA DARDER

Routledge
Taylor & Francis Group

NEW YORK AND LONDON

KH

First published 2015
by Routledge
711 Third Avenue, New York, NY 10017

Simultaneously published in the UK
by Routledge
2 Park Square, Milton Park, Abingdon, Oxon OX14 4RN

Routledge is an imprint of the Taylor & Francis Group, an informa business

Library of Congress Cataloging-in-Publication Data
A catalog record for this book is available from the Library of Congress

ISBN: 978-0-415-53839-8 (hbk)
ISBN: 978-0-415-53840-4 (pbk)
ISBN: 978-0-203-10902-1 (ebk)

Typeset in Minion
by Apex CoVantage, LLC

Printed and bound in the United States of America by
Edwards Brothers Malloy on sustainably sourced paper

3/2/16

DEDICATION

This book is lovingly dedicated to the memory of Paulo
Freire, whom I will always call *my father in the struggle,*
for his contribution to my full political awakening and
the revolutionary spirit of freedom and hope that his
love instilled in me.

Este livro é carinhosamente dedicado à memória de
Paulo Freire, a quem eu sempre vou chamar o meu pai na
luta, pela sua contribuição para o meu despertar político
completo eo espírito revolucionário de liberdade e esperança
de que o seu amor incutiu em mim.

I am a teacher who favors the permanent struggle against every form of bigotry and against the economic domination of individuals and social classes. I am a teacher who rejects the present system of capitalism, responsible for the aberration of misery in the midst of plenty. I am a teacher full of the spirit of hope, in spite of all the signs to the contrary.

Paulo Freire
Pedagogy of Freedom (1998a)

CONTENTS

SERIES EDITOR INTRODUCTION   VIII

PREFACE   IX

ACKNOWLEDGMENTS   XIV

1   Liberation: Our Historical Task   1

2   Pedagogy of Love: Embodying Our Humanity   47

3   Conscientizaçao: Awakening Critical Consciousness   80

4   Problematizing Diversity: A Dialogue with Paulo Freire   132

Epilogue   Our Struggle Continues   166

REFERENCES   173

INDEX   177

SERIES EDITOR INTRODUCTION

This series introduces key people and topics and discusses their particular implications for the field of education. Written by the most prominent thinkers in the field, these "key ideas" are read through the series' authors' past and present work, with particular attention given to the ways these ideas can, do, and might impact theory, research, practice, and policy in education.

More specifically, these texts offer particular conversations with prominent authors, whose work has resonated across education and related fields. Books in this series read as conversations with authorities, whose thinking has helped constitute these ideas and their role in the field of education—yesterday, today, and tomorrow.

Much more than introductions alone, these short, virtuosic volumes look to shape ongoing discussions in the field of education by putting the field's contemporary luminaries in dialogue with its foundational figures and critical topics. From new students to senior scholars, these volumes will spark the imaginations of a range of readers thinking through key ideas and education.

Greg Dimitriadis and Bob Lingard

PREFACE

It is necessary that the weakness of the powerless is transformed into a force capable of announcing justice.

—Paulo Freire (1970b)

The purpose of this book is not to provide a systematic analysis of Paulo Freire's work. Over 100 scholarly books have been written specifically about Freire's philosophy, pedagogy, and his life. Moreover, the purpose of this book series is to provide readers with a particular understanding of how contemporary theorists have engaged, in a personal way, the work of historical intellectuals, who have richly influenced their own theories of education. Hence, this is what this book is meant to provide readers—a tiny picture of the ways in which Freire's writings have informed my own scholarship and the places in his work from which I springboard to reinvent and expand my particular articulation of his contribution to the world. I begin here, because, as is so common on the left, we seem to always be seeking a yet more perfect argument or crystallizing insight or distinct theoretical formulation of past work, through tearing apart even the efforts of those who are our true comrades. So it is important that I dispel from the onset false expectations and, instead, stand solidly on the ground of a critical intersubjectivity.

This book then is about the ways in which Paulo Freire's work has personally had an influence on my life and my scholarship in education. The hope is that this contribution to the literature can help young scholars, in a larger way, to understand that the forces of our lived histories and personal proclivities are seldom absent from the theorists we choose to follow or, for that matter, those we disavow. And, as such, we all bring a different perspective to the table about their work and contributions. In many ways, it is precisely these differences, in our reading, interpretations, or reinventions of Freire, for example, which can move us toward developing a greater sensibility of what it means to live a critically intellectual and socially democratic life, as an embodied phenomenon of consciousness and struggle—a phenomenon where a multiplicity of perspectives must find a common place to anchor, and a common place to anchor that retains the capacity to hold the multiplicity.

As such, I do not set out here to provide you the definitive reading of Paulo Freire and his contributions to education, but rather to share with you the manner in which his writings have illuminated my life practices and my thinking, as a working class, educator of color in the United States, who has actively struggled, in a myriad of ways, to overcome the impact of my colonization and disempowerment, as a Puerto Rican woman born within U.S. colonialism and reared as a child of the diaspora. Yet, this is not an autobiography, but rather an analysis of solidarity, in mind, heart, and spirit, with one of the most powerful and revolutionary educational philosophers of the 20th century—who was also an important emissary of hope and possibility.

True to Freire's words, my scholarship has deliberately entailed a tireless effort to transform "the weakness of my powerlessness" into "a force capable of announcing justice." And as such, this is a very particular perspective, told through the power of Freirian thought. Similarly, I trust that each person, who has been influenced by Paulo Freire's work, no matter his or her history, also has his or her own story to tell. In my case, I seek to tell a story of Freire's work, anchored within the dialectics of his critical philosophy and pedagogy, while simultaneously grounded culturally, politically, economically, and ideologically within my own revolutionary praxis of love, dignity, and class struggle.

As inferred earlier, much has been written about Paulo Freire over the last four decades. Scholars have focused on many different aspects of Freire's idea and his pedagogy. Often the emphasis has been on Freire's articulation of dialogue and its relationship to a problem-posing pedagogy, the dynamics of the oppressor-oppressed dialectic, issues of banking education, or a rationale for understanding literacy as an emancipatory force that must be well situated in the lived histories of the people. In addition to these philosophical concerns, Freire also spoke to critical questions tied to the transformation of consciousness (or *conscientizaçao*) and leadership, which are less well discussed. Nevertheless, these are also significant to both educational and community leadership practices committed to the struggle for social justice, human rights, and economic democracy.

Hence, I have sought to articulate the manner in which Freire's writings contributed to educational and community efforts related to my own development as an activist-scholar and given the moment in history when the book was first released. That is, I have worked to contextualize Freire's early work within the revolutionary struggles that were waged during the late 1960s and early 1970s, when the book first began to circulate in progressive teacher and community circles in the United States. Given my personal history as an impoverished and colonized subject, my desire is to link Freire's work to the larger struggles of communities of color, in response to a long history of racism and economic apartheid, placing importance on the spirit of consciousness and its impact on the transformation of material life.

Through this effort, I invite readers to consider Paulo Freire, the man, humanist, educator, and revolutionary intellectual of faith and love, as I came to understand him—not with reverence or idolatry, but rather as a human being, like each of us, who lived his life committed persistently to the emancipation of the most disenfranchised and to the reinvention of education—beyond the repressive forces and furtive violence of education under capitalism. Whether he accomplished this task or not is not my concern here for I do not believe that Freire considered his work with an endpoint but rather a contribution to the long historical struggle for human emancipation. As such, this book entails my dialogical engagement with Freire's ideas, anchored in my cultural understanding, politics, and lived history as a Boricua. It is from this vantage point that I have attempted to engage with those Freirian ideas that most speak to my work, in an effort to be true to Freire's intent—that we engage, extend, and reinvent his pedagogical treatise in ways that are genuinely organic, salient, and empowering to our own lives and practice, both as individuals and communal beings.

So this book is not born from the typical objective and distanced epistemological gaze of the traditional theorist, but rather from an engaged, contextual, and relational dance of identifying, knowing, and experiencing in the world. Moreover, I leave the task of intellectual judgments and analytical cutting to those more erudite scholars, who feel fully equipped to lay down such claims. Rather, I seek to illustrate humbly how Freire's practice exemplifies the courageous spirit of determination and restless grappling with complexities that must fully permeate our conscious efforts to transform the politics and practice of education in this country and abroad—and by so doing, honor Paulo Freire's (2005) soulful intent: "I hope at least the following will endure: my trust in the people, and my faith in men and women, and in the creation of a world in which it will be easier to love" (p. 40).

Antonia Darder
Loyola Marymount University
Los Angeles, CA

ACKNOWLEDGMENTS

I want to acknowledge here some of the people that have been essential to the writing of this book. First, I want to thank Catherine Bernard, my editor at Routledge, who approached me to write this book. I am humbled and honored by her trust and value in my scholarship, for truly there are so many greater scholars who could have easily written this book. But then, it would have been a very different story.

I am, particularly, grateful to my friend, Rodolfo D. Torres, who has also been an ever-present intellectual colleague and political comrade for more than 25 years. His consistent fellowship and support have been truly essential to my survival as a working class woman of color, forging through the morass of university politics—an arena that still effectively reproduces power dynamics steeped in elitism, racism, and sexism, while it attempts to squelch the lives of those who speak truth to power.

I am also forever in debt to Carol Brunson Day, Louise Derman-Sparks, Barbara Richardson, Henry Giroux, Rodolfo Torres, Peter McLaren, and Donaldo Macedo for contributing to my development as a scholar; and to Paulo and Nita Freire who during imperceptible social moments taught me about the power, coherence, love, and wisdom to be gleaned from our lived histories of survival.

Similarly, I am thankful to so many other radical colleagues (too many to name here, but you know who you are) and students who have, over the years, been willing to persist in deep conversations and academic collaborations with me, in an effort to push the boundaries of university legitimacy, in our struggle and commitment to work *with* students and communities to forge a more just world.

Lastly, I am most grateful for my children, my grandchildren, family, friends, and community; for without them all, I would be nothing but an aimless, lonely creature, isolated from the greatest gift of all—the power of unconditional love.

1

LIBERATION: OUR
HISTORICAL TASK

The greatest humanistic and historical task of the oppressed: to
liberate themselves . . .

—Paulo Freire (1970b)

More than 40 years after *Pedagogy of the Oppressed* was first
released, the inequalities and injustices that Paulo Freire was
addressing then continue to persist in the United States and
around the world today. In many instances, these conditions
have only worsened in the last two decades, with the steady
infusion of neoliberal imperatives into education, focused on
privatization, deregulation, and free-market enterprise. With
this in mind, it is important to begin any discussion on the
legacy of Freire here; in that, often, it has been precisely Freire's
revolutionary critique of capitalism and the relationship of

schooling to class formation that have been systematically stripped away, resulting in diluted versions of his ideas.

As a scholar of color who was born in Puerto Rico, a colonized subject, and reared in the urban poverty of the United States, it is impossible to convince me, given my lived history, that oppression's center of gravity for those of us deemed as "other" is simply the psychological aberration (or micro aggressions) perpetrated by White people toward our so-called race. Rather, I argue that the processes that reproduce racism at all levels of the society, including education, are intimately connected to the material domination and exploitation of our communities by the powerful elite—and enacted, for the most part, by those who are not themselves affluent, but answer daily its siren call.

Although seldom spoken or acknowledged in traditional discourses about Freire's work, there are particular ways in which radical Black, Latino, Native American, and Asian-American working class communities of the 1960s and 1970s embraced his revolutionary ideas and pedagogical assertions. Freire's observation, in contrast, acknowledged this phenomenon, when responding to those who deemed his work metaphysical, abstract, or dense: "Workers also understand my work, as well as those who have some experience of oppression. But I acknowledge there might be a problem of cross-cultural translation with [more privileged and mainstream] U.S. readers."[1]

For many of us, Freire (2002) was one of the few philosophical educational theorists of the time that inspired us to struggle: "[We] were on fire with the love of freedom, and had found a point of reference in *Pedagogy of the Oppressed*" (p. 184). The distinctiveness of his radical discourse spoke to a grounded understanding of our racialized oppression and powerfully linked us to a larger international anti-imperialist struggle taking place around the world. In other words, if we were to counter the impact of the historical and contemporary impact of genocide, slavery, and colonialism, we had to begin by engaging the manner in which racism is inextricably tied to imperatives of social class formation and material exclusion. Freire (2005) contended that although "one cannot reduce the analysis of racism to social class, one cannot understand racism fully without a class analysis, for to do one at the expense of the other is to fall prey into a sectarianist position, which is as despicable as the racism that we need to reject" (p. 15).

Freire's work then was central to understanding movement strategies related to community struggles, educational politics, and theoretical formations, in that he specifically grounded his analysis in an understanding of poverty as oppression and capitalism as the root of domination. The struggle for radical activist of color was not foremost about "celebrating diversity," identity politics, or cultural legitimacy, but rather, it was a larger struggle for our humanity and our survival, given that we had suffered, in the flesh, the violence of oppression at every level of our existence. Hence, the more radical arms of the civil rights era recognized that local political struggles for self-determination had to also be connected to a larger international political project of class struggle and an incisive critique of capitalism, racism, and patriarchy. During that short-lived era, movement organizations of color came to understand their struggle within the context of a long history shaped by the violence of colonialism. Important links were made between the economic imperatives that led to the colonization of the land, exploitation of workers, and the enslavement of African-Americans. As such, we recognized that the purpose of our engagement with Freire's work was as much about unveiling the structures of domination as it was about decolonizing our minds of hegemonic ideologies that made us complicit with our oppression.

Freire's philosophical insights about the oppressor/oppressed contradiction and its internalization among oppressed populations was echoed by writers of color of the 20th century, who spoke to this phenomenon in their political articulations of the plights of impoverished racialized communities. Many authors of color also made references to a dual process of socialization, not found in ethnocentric theories of the dominant culture. In concert with Freire's (1985) understanding, "without a sense of identity, there can be no real struggle" (p. 186), theorists of color sought to better comprehend and posit theories of identity. These perspectives challenged Eurocentric epistemologies, notions of identity, and Western concepts of human development. Theorist of color, instead, spoke to the phenomenon of double consciousness, double vision, bicultural identity, diunital consciousness, multidimensional consciousness, duality, of our twin beings, and so on (Darder, 2012), referring to the collision of not only two cultures but of deep asymmetrical relations of powers, which led to the subordination and erasure of our histories and material oppression of our communities. Restoring the integrity of our voices and centering our cultural and historical knowledge of survival, in sync with Freire's pedagogy, became an important political quest, in an era where our voices and participation remained relatively silent and absent from the spheres of power.

As a young woman, meeting Paulo Freire, hearing him speak, and reading his work truly changed the course of my life, as an educator and political activist. This was for many reasons, of course. However, what cannot be denied is that this was partly so because he looked and felt more like people from my own community—people exiled by colonialism from or within our own lands. At the time, he was exiled from Brazil for his emancipatory literacy efforts with poor populations from the Brazilian countryside—those whom he credited for much of his ideas for *Pedagogy of the Oppressed*. Freire often spoke of his work as a manifestation of what he had learned through his relationship with those who were the most dispossessed in his country. His writings generated in activists and educators of color, in the United States and other parts of the world, greater political clarity and commitment.

Freire's writings also challenged educators to truly embody our commitment to political consciousness and social transformation, within the everyday relationships we forged with those within and outside our cultural communities. What we understood was that *pedagogy of the oppressed* was not pedagogy solely for the classroom, but rather a living pedagogy that has to be infused into all aspects of our lives, including our personal politics. This is to say that *teaching to transgress* had to constitute a moral stance, often belittled and diminished within mainstream political discourses, even on the left. So much so that it caused bell hooks (1994) to write, "It always astounds me when progressive people act as though it is somehow a naive moral position to believe that our lives must be a living example of our politics" (p. 48).

For communities betrayed by our schooling, Freire's message promised the possibility of an educational project for our children tied to a larger political democratic vision—one that resonated with our anticolonial struggles for self-determination and political aspirations to become full subjects of our histories, as well as control our own destinies. Pedagogy of the oppressed also signaled a pedagogy of transgression—transgression of oppressive ideologies, attitudes, structures, conditions, and practices within education and society that debilitate our humanity. It is not surprising that Freire's humanistic inclinations and political vision of education resonated deeply with movement demands of educators and activists of color who sought fundamental change to the process of schooling in this country and those societal structures that worked against the emancipatory interests of our children and our communities.

Through Freire's (1970b) ideas, we came to acknowledge that education can serve as an important vehicle for the political formation of citizens within a democratic society. This pointed to a humanizing educational process that could prepare students from oppressed communities for voice, participation in civil society, and ethical decision making in all aspects of their life. A central political aim of such a humanizing process of education is to support the evolution of critical consciousness with an explicit aim toward the establishment of a more harmonious and peaceful world. Starting from the fundamental realization that we live in an unequal world, an emancipatory pedagogy had to encompass a collective "struggle for our humanization, for the emancipation of labor, and for the overcoming of our alienation" (p. 28), so that we might affirm ourselves as full political subjects of our lives.

Freire (1970b) articulated a vision that he considered "an indispensable condition for the quest for human completion" (p. 31)—a completion that although would remain ever unfinished, nevertheless could enliven our imagination, creativity, hope, and commitment to resist the forces of domination and exploitation within education and the larger society. For Freire, freedom encompassed our human capacity "to be" and to exist authentically. Moreover, our capacity to live free required a fundamental shift in how we defined ourselves and the conditions in which we exist. This entailed a humanizing process that could support and facilitate the ongoing development of critical consciousness, so that we might find the cognitive, emotional, psychological, and spiritual strength necessary to critique and denounce conditions of oppression, embrace a life of solidarity, and announce new possibilities for a more just world.

Toward this end, Freire (1970b) understood that our task as teachers and students is to embrace a historical understanding of our relationship with the world and transform our teaching and learning into revolutionary praxis—a sound political pedagogy of "reflection and action upon the world to transform it" (p. 36). He argued that it is imperative that we, as educators, work in our communities to unveil and challenge the contradictions of educational policies and practices that objectify and dehumanize us, preventing our expression as full subjects of history. Indeed such a vision of education entails an ongoing political process. One that can only be sustained through collective labor—a labor born of love, but deeply anchored in an unceasing commitment to know, through both theory and practice, the nature of the beast that preys on our humanity.

Education as a Political Act

> Education is part and parcel of the very nature of education . . . It does not matter where or when it has taken place, whether it is more or less complex, education has always been a political act.
>
> —Paulo Freire (1993)

Freire (1993) was clear and forthright about his belief in the political nature of education. Furthermore, he believed that our political definition of our pedagogical orientation in the classroom and communities had to be understood explicitly with respect to our political responsibility as social agents for change. This view rips apart assumptions of neutrality in education, in that it demands from educators that we clearly take on our labor as a political act, defining ourselves "either in favor of freedom, living it authentically, or against it" (p. 64). Freire's personal enactment of this important principle in his work was made obvious when he wrote,

> In the name of the respect I should have for my students, I do not see why I should omit or hide my political stance by proclaiming a neutral position that does not exist. On the contrary, my role as teacher is to assent the student's right to compare, to choose, to rupture, to decide.
>
> (p. 68)

Thus, within the context of education, whether we are conscious of it or not, Freire recognized that all educators perpetuate political values, beliefs, myths, and meanings about the world. As such, education has to be understood as a politicizing (or depoliticizing) institutional process that conditions students to ascribe to the dominant ideological norms and epistemological assumptions of the prevailing social order. In addition, Freire helped us to understand how the hegemonic culture of schooling socializes students to accept their particular role or place within the material order—a role or place that historically has been determined by the colonizing forces of the dominant society, based on the political economy and its sorted structures of oppression. What Freire's writings made clear to educators and activists was that schools are enmeshed in the political economy of the society and at its service. As such, schools are political sites involved in the construction, control, and containment of oppressed cultural populations, through their legitimating function, with respect to discourse, meaning, and subjectivity. And, furthermore, "the more [we] deny the political dimension of education, the more [we] assume the moral potential to blame the victims" (Freire & Macedo, 1987, p. 123).

Freire's pedagogy of the oppressed courageously discarded an uncritical acceptance of the prevailing social order and its structures of capitalist exploitation, embracing the empowerment of dispossessed populations as the primary purpose of liberatory education. In essence, his revolutionary praxis turned the traditional purpose of public education on its proverbial head, to unveil its contradictions. Instead of educating students to become simply reliable workers, complacent citizens, and avid consumers, Freire called upon educators to engage students in a critical understanding of *the world* in order to consider emancipatory possibilities, born from the lived histories and material conditions that shaped their daily lives. Freire's (1993) common use of "the world" here is important to grasp, in that its meaning was both material and ideological, not merely poetic metaphor. Rather he explained:

> When I speak of the world, I am not speaking exclusively about the trees and the animals that I love very much, and the mountains and rivers. I am not speaking exclusively of nature which I am a part, but I am speaking also of the social structures, politics, culture, history, of which I am also a part.
>
> (p. 103)

This perspective of classroom and community life helped us to understand how historically, as a consequence of cultural and linguistic colonization and economic subjugation, populations of color in this country and abroad have been systematically oppressed. For more than 40 years, this knowledge has helped to support radical educators in unveiling those hidden ideological values and beliefs that inform standardized curricula, materials, textbooks, testing and assessment, promotion criteria, and institutional relationships, in an effort to support and better infuse our teaching with an emancipatory political vision of schools and community life. In so doing, we came to recognize that the task at hand is not to reproduce the traditional social arrangements that support and perpetuate inequality and injustice, but rather, to work toward the transformation of these conditions, within the context of our vocation as human beings and our daily efforts as educators and community activists committed to social change.

For Freire (1970b), schools are inextricably linked to the hegemonic process of cultural, political, and economic life. He theorized that it is precisely these processes of domination that reinforce and give legitimacy to the reproduction of a "banking" system of education. The reflection of the dominant class and culture is inscribed in the educational policies and practices that shape hegemonic schooling. One of the most pervasive aspects of this approach has been the instrumentalizing practice of teaching-to-the-test. This sterile and enfeebling pedagogical approach functions to "minimize or annul students' creative power and stimulate their credulity" (p. 60) so as to reinforce intellectual submissiveness and conformity to the state's prescribed ideological definition of legitimate knowledge and academic measures of achievement.

Freire (1970b) denounced instrumentalizing forms of pedagogy, given that these perpetuate cultural values of domination by teaching students they exist "abstract, isolated, independent and unattached to the world, that the world exists as a reality apart" (p. 69) from their control or influence. This deceptively and effectively works to structure the silences of students of color by relegating them to objects of their learning. Furthermore, this bankrupt logic of standardization adheres to a political message of conformity, which renders suspect social critique, particularly from those deemed deficient and unworthy to speak.

In powerful ways, Freire's pedagogical project assisted us to expose how most teachers are simply not prepared to critique the destructive impacts of disabling practices in schools nor able to support students in their political formation. Hence, alienated and powerless to challenge the oppressive apparatus of schooling that mythologizes the authoritarianism of standardized knowledge and curricula, teachers become complicit in concealing the class formation and colonizing role of schools. Over the years, "scientific" myths attached to the need for high-stakes testing, standardized knowledge, and meritocracy have only solidified in the popular imagination. Seasonal publication of test scores in local newspapers has been used to rank the achievement status of teachers and schools. This public exposition has placed increasing federal and state pressure on school districts; pressure that school district officials displace upon principals; which principals, in turn, displace on teachers; and teachers on their students and parents.

Freire's politics of education, in sync with our lived histories, highlighted for educators and activists of color how classroom practices often replicate similar fears, frustrations, and insecurities that mirror those of their students, when they hit unfamiliar territory and receive little substantive support in the process of their everyday practice. Consequently, educators experience enormous constraints due to the system of reward and punishment commonly employed by administrators to control teacher labor. This is reflected in the authoritarian manner in which school administrators can limit the decision-making role of teachers, through prescribing rules for dress, conduct, curricula, textbooks, lesson plans, classroom activities, student assessment, and the nature of parent participation. Freire (1998b) spoke to the political impact of prescribed behavior on teaching practice:

> Teachers become fearful; they begin to internalize the dominator's shadow and authoritarian ideology of the administration. These teachers are no longer with their students because the force of the punishment and threatening dominant ideology comes between them . . . In other words, they are forbidden to be.
>
> (p. 9)

Freire (1998b) also linked the destructive impact of the traditional punishment and rewards system to the politics of teacher evaluation. He highlighted the unfortunate manner in which traditional teacher evaluation methods tend to focus less on the teacher's practice and far more on evaluating the teacher's "personality"—namely the teacher's willingness to conform and comply to traditional roles and expectations. As a consequence, "we evaluate to punish and almost never to improve teacher's practice. In other words, we evaluate to punish and not educate" (p. 7). Freire, however, was not opposed to the practice of teacher evaluation. On the contrary, he firmly argued that "the evaluation of practice represents an important and indispensable factor" (p. 7) in the development of teaching practice, but it had to be grounded in a participatory approach if it was to be a useful tool in supporting the ongoing critical formation of educators. Anything short of this grounded approach results in a domesticating process that thwarts teacher responsibility, while rendering them ambiguous and indecisive. Freire asserted that this ambiguity and indecisiveness often leads us to grasp at "a false sense of security . . . informed by the paternalistic nurturing" (p. 6) with which teachers are rewarded for their conformity.

In order to break out of the contradiction of false security, Freire urged us to establish collective relationships of struggle, in order to interrogate openly the consequences of educational practices and to consider more effective strategies for disrupting the political domestication that inanimate the intellectual and political formation of students from oppressed communities. Freire (1998b) considered that such collective empowerment reinforced the need for teachers to struggle together in identifying,

> . . . the tactical paths that competent and politically clear teachers must follow . . . to critically reject their domesticating role; in so doing they affirm themselves as teachers by demythologizing the authoritarianism of teaching packages and their administration in the intimacy of their world, which is also the world of their students. In their classroom, with the doors closed, it is difficult to have their world unveiled.
>
> (p. 9)

Freire's political understanding of teaching was deeply rooted in a democratic view of education as a permanent terrain of struggle, resistance, and transformation. The common perception of public schooling as a neutral or benevolent enterprise therefore is categorically dismissed. However, given the long history of conflicts and contradictions at work in the ideological formation of educational institutions in an ostensibly democratic nation like the United States, Freire's politics of education also guided us in recognizing that seldom has domination been absolutely deterministic in its reproduction. Wherever oppression exists, there also exist side-by-side the seeds for resistance, at different stages of expression and evolution. Freire's pedagogy of the oppressed nourished and cultivated the seeds of our political resistance—a resistance that we could link historically to a multitude of collective struggles waged around the world in efforts to genuinely democratize education and societies. Our pedagogical process of political empowerment, then and now, entails a long historical process—where our struggle in schools constitutes a significant political front.

Knowledge as Historical Process

> Through their continuing praxis, men and women simultaneously create history and become historical-social beings . . . their history, in function of their own creations, develops as a constant process of transformation . . . Were this [not] the case, a fundamental condition of history—its continuity—would disappear.
>
> —Paulo Freire (1970b)

Freire asserted that a critical understanding of history and ourselves as historical subjects is fundamental to a revolutionary praxis. Yet, most educators have traditionally been socialized to think of history as frozen and fixed. For most teachers, history is a subject taught from a book about things that happened in the past—this points to a passive and reified notion of history that disembodies the oppressed, excluding our active participants in the making of history. To counter this debilitating view, Freire repeatedly noted that knowledge is the product of a historical process. Who we are and how we come to know the world is profoundly influenced by the particular historical events that shape our understanding of the world, at any given moment in time. By the same token, our collective responses to events also alter the course of history, as well. In this light, Freire (1998a) wrote,

> Even before I read Marx, I had made his words my own. I had taken my own radical stance on the defense of the legitimate interest of the human person. There is no theory of socio-political transformation that moves me if it is not grounded in an understanding of the human person as a maker of history and as one made by history.
>
> (p. 115)

From this empowering view of history, we also came to comprehend knowledge as a widely plural and partial phenomenon, constructed under a variety of material conditions, subject positions, geographical locations, and epochal formations. Yet, neither is this plurality or partiality of history acknowledged in the teaching of history nor are the hegemonic structures of power, which determine whose historical account will be preserved as official public record. In contrast, Freire posited that historical accounts of the dominant culture are deeply mired in the political and economic interests of the ruling class. Official historical accounts of the dominant society then do not miraculously appear within a vacuum, neutral and untarnished by ideology and material aims. Instead, all readings of history are constructed within a set of values and beliefs that shape the ontological and epistemological interpretations given to particular societal relationships and events. Freire (1970b) called for a critical perspective to unveil the dialectical tensions that are hidden underneath, in that "historical themes are never isolated, independent, disconnected or static; they are always interacting dialectically with their opposites" (pp. 91–92).

Understanding history from this vantage point sheds light on the whitewashed partiality and limitations of officially recorded accounts of history and, furthermore, reveals the historical absences of the oppressed who remained exiled and suppressed by *epistemicides* of power (Paraskeva, 2011). Through naming outright this historical injustice, Freire's vision reinforced the need for oppressed communities to recover and uncover our documented and undocumented histories, which have remained hidden from mainstream life. Nevertheless, Freire believed that one important place to begin the labor of uncovering the lived histories of oppressed populations is within the classroom.

To discover ourselves as historical beings constituted for Freire a significant emancipatory moment in the lived histories of the oppressed. He firmly believed that when we come to see ourselves as capable of affecting the course of history through our collective voices and actions, this emancipatory process also assists us to fend off the hopelessness of oppression. Educators, students, and communities working together gain greater insight into the historical process, by way of their collective efforts to name and change the world. In naming the world and constructing meaning, we begin to experience what it means to be subjects of our own lives; and through acting upon the world in meaningful ways, students from oppressed communities develop voice and social agency. Discovering this sense of being a subject of history and becoming comfortable in exercising our social agency constituted for Freire (1970b) a significant liberatory process to the political formation of self-determination and community empowerment—both indispensable to our struggle for liberation.

Freire associated the historicity of knowledge with epochal shifts in the world that require our praxis to evolve, in sync with the new conditions that we must confront. Each epoch or era is defined by new historical circumstances and accompanying events that may require very different political strategies, tactics, or pacts than those of the past. This is to say that our work must draw from the events and lessons of the past, but also consistently work to *reinvent* unjust conditions, in order to remain grounded in the present needs of students and their communities. This critical approach is extended and deepened through our pedagogy, when we embrace a dialectical view of knowledge, history, and the world. It is, moreover, through our capacity to observe and interpret what Freire (1970b) called *limit-situations* and to engage these objectively, alongside the historical conditions that inform them, that provides us new knowledge from which to make liberating decisions, within our classroom and communities. Of this, Freire (1970b) wrote,

> . . . as they locate the seat of their decisions in themselves and in their relations with the world and others, people overcome the situations which limit them: the "limit-situations." Once perceived by individuals as fetters, as obstacles to their liberation, these situations stand out in relief from the background, revealing their true nature as concrete historical dimensions of a given reality.
>
> (p. 99)

For Freire, the world exists as it does because of the multitude of relationships and structures, historical and contemporary, constructed by human beings, of which we are all a part. And, as such, our vision for transforming schools and society are not only plausible, but absolutely possible. We learned from Freire that to instill such radical hope in our students and communities required that we too be absolutely convinced of our right to struggle and to be sincerely committed to our revolutionary dreams.

Similarly, knowledge as a historical phenomenon implies that it emerges out of communal processes, produced dynamically, though our relationships with one another and the world. As noted earlier, Freire viewed emancipatory knowledge as a living process—a living historical process that grows and transforms within an environment of teaching and learning that is informed by a critical epistemological commitment to dialogue and the evolution of social consciousness. Here, Freire's (Freire & Macedo, 1995) notion of the dialogical must be understood as a relational way of knowing and being in communion with others, not manipulation or coercion.

> Dialogue is a way of knowing and should never be viewed as a mere tactic to involve students in a particular task. We have to make this point very clear. I engage in dialogue not necessarily because I like the other person. I engage in dialogue because I recognize the social and not merely the individualistic character of the process of knowing. In this sense, dialogue presents itself as an indispensable component of the process of both learning and knowing.
>
> (p. 379)

This relational understanding of dialogue is, again, in direct opposition to banking education, which predominantly anchors ideas of teaching and learning to values of individualism, independence, and competition. For this reason, Freire placed great emphasis on dialogue as an epistemological practice. He believed that only through love and trust, which generates and is generated by dialogue, could teachers and students come to know the world critically, recovering the power to transform our lives as historical subjects.

The Dialectical Relationship

> Humans, however, because they are aware of themselves and thus of the world—because they are conscious beings—exist in a dialectical relationship between the determination of limits and their own freedom.
>
> —Paulo Freire (1970b)

Freire upheld in his work the importance of the dialectical relationship—that relational tension between seemingly opposites—as necessary to the critical process of consciousness and the construction of emancipatory knowledge. This radical perspective compels us to engage critically with those social and material conditions that emerge from the ideological differences in cultural values and beliefs, as well as asymmetrical relations of power that repress them. Again, also important here are the ways that limit-situations, which stem from such tensions, can also serve as unexpected creative venues in our pedagogical and political efforts. That is, through our openness to exploring limit-situations, critiquing the existing tensions and consequences, we can also create the means by which critical knowledge is constructed within particular historical moments. In other words, new knowledge forms result from our dialectical engagement with the historical and contemporary tensions that call forth new possibilities.

When dialectical tensions expressed as resistance to structures of domination are suppressed within traditional classrooms or communities, the critical reflection, dialogue, and action necessary for emancipatory knowledge are thwarted.

Accordingly, students of color, who experience tremendous tensions due to conflicting values and beliefs between the classroom curriculum and their daily lives, are often silenced by mainstream values and expectations of schooling that curtail their participation. A revolutionary practice, on the other hand, strives to stretch the limited boundaries of what is considered permissible discourse, in order to create the pedagogical conditions for students to engage freely across their lived histories in the process of knowledge construction. By stretching the boundaries of what is deemed acceptable discourse and legitimate knowledge, educators construct counter-hegemonic or transgressive spaces that shatter the *culture of silence* (Freire, 2002). In so doing, the democratic potential of students who have been historically excluded from participation is nurtured.

Freire also linked this dialectical understanding of knowledge construction to the notion of ideology, for how we construct knowledge is directly connected to the set of values and beliefs we employ to make sense of the world. Yet, our ideological belief systems generally exist most steadfastly within the realm of unexamined assumptions, which are preserved by way of a historical commonsense (Gramsci, 1971). These antidialectical assumptions about the world generally impact our attitudes and practices about why we believe people are poor; what we think it means to be a person of color; the attitudes we hold about children and their rights; how we articulate the differences between men and woman; our views about God or spirituality; and what we perceive to be legitimate power relations within schools. Then, based on these underlying assumptions, we formulate pedagogical decisions about student expectations, classroom materials, interaction with students and parents, and expressions of authority in the classroom.

The issue of authority in the classroom is worth greater discussion. Within the context of schooling, most well-meaning teachers—particularly those working with working class students of color—consider "strictness" a legitimate expression of teacher authority. However, often their discourse is mired by an authoritarian rhetoric of student control and containment "for their own good." In the process, the dialectical relationship between authority and freedom is negated. In contrast, Freire (2002) summons up the contradiction by which true freedom evolves, by arguing "there is no freedom without authority, there is no authority without freedom" (p. 21). His perspective retains the dialectical tension between authority and freedom, which reinforces the communal value and need for limits, if we are to exist in a genuinely democratic world. In *Pedagogy of the City,* Freire (1993) wrote,

> To create a practice of a democratic nature—a practice in which we learn how to deal with the tension between authority and freedom, a tension that cannot be avoided unless through the sacrifice of democracy . . . the more authentically I live the tension, the less I fear freedom and the less I reject the necessary authority.
>
> (p. 130)

Freire's view, moreover, refers to a process in which *both* teachers and students must enter into dialogue as subjects, with responsibility for the context created. As such, teachers have responsibility to use their authority to create conditions where students are free to read their world, according to the authority of their lived histories and from there construct new knowledge. Given the uncanny manner that unexamined assumptions and beliefs about the world unexpectedly creep into our pedagogy, it is imperative that critical educators reflect often on their practice of authority and their educational decisions. To do so helps teachers to uncover contradictions that may inadvertently obstruct our efforts to construct a liberatory practice and thus, make different choices. Freire (1998b) saw this process as an ongoing and necessary one for revolutionary educators striving toward greater coherence in our practice. In the struggle for coherence between what we say and do, Freire urged us to diminish the distance. However, he also acknowledged that it is not possible to be absolutely consistent, but rather, through moments of inconsistency, we are challenged to reflect anew upon our ambiguities.

> In the moment that I discover the inconsistency between what I say and what I do—progressive discourse, authoritarian practice—if, reflecting, at times painfully, I learn the ambiguity in which I find myself, I feel I am not able to continue like this and I look for a way out. In this way, a new choice is imposed on me. Either I change the progressive discourse for a discourse consistent with my reactionary practice, or I change my practice for a democratic one.
>
> (p. 67)

Given the covert manner that the political economy impacts the control of knowledge within classroom, educators must align their practice with a democratic intent. Through the courage to pose difficult questions, expose the tensions, and refuse to fall into the complacency of privilege, teachers are in a key position to support new readings of the world and participate in unveiling the hidden faces of oppression. Moreover, to enliven democracy in the classroom, Freire (1997) argued that we had to nurture relationships of dialogue and solidarity within schools and communities—relationships grounded in our unwavering fidelity to break out of the domesticating conditions and institutional structures that dehumanize our lives and entrap us within a political economy that is primarily fueled by avarice, greed, and indifference.

Schooling and Capitalism

> Brutalizing the workforce by subjecting them to routine procedures is part of the nature of the capitalist mode of production. And what is taking place in the production of knowledge in the schools is in large part a reproduction of that mechanism.
>
> —Paulo Freire (in Freire & Faundez, 1989)

Freire, in no uncertain terms, saw capitalism as the root of oppression. He often made direct references to the logic of capitalism, with its debilitating impact on workers and the need to override the consumerism of the marketplace. Freire offered us a critical analysis of schooling situated firmly against the dynamics of capitalist accumulation and the reproduction of a deeply racialized and gendered labor force. He contended that the politics of schooling, informed by the economic interests of the ruling class, supports the reproduction of inequality, by replicating "the authoritarianism of the capitalist mode of production" (Freire & Macedo, 1998, p. 229). The impact of the political economy on the educational conditions of students from racialized communities is made visible in a variety of ways, including the types of academic expectations, financial resources, and other opportunities available to them, which contrast dramatically to those of affluent student populations.

Unfortunately for the majority of people, this distinction is seldom engaged beyond the belief that if a family can afford to pay for an excellent education for their children, then they deserve the privilege. In contrast, the majority of students from economically oppressed communities are positioned within schools, according to their class location within the racialized economic order. Meanwhile, blatant structural inequalities are successfully camouflaged by the myths that place exaggerated weight on "exceptional" success stories, despite the fact that only a small percentage of individuals from poor communities manage ever to achieve social mobility, despite educational attainment. Commonly repeated myths such as "education leads to social mobility" conceal, according to Freire (1997), "the class war raging throughout the country . . . a class war that hides and makes confusing a frustrated class struggle" (p. 50).

As a consequence, the class structure has remained unchanged during the last 70 years. Teachers bridled by the myth that the United States is a classless society, blindly perpetuate contradictory teaching practices that deepen the structures of class inequality. In an effort to challenge glaring economic contradictions and the myths that sustain them, Freire proposed a pedagogy that would help to make visible and explicit issues of social class and its impact on schooling. For example, the class-bound arrangement of public schools has existed since their inception. Public schools designed to function as factories of learning for the future workers of the nation have sought to insure their consensual participation in the process of capitalist accumulation. The majority of public school students were expected to move into a file-and-rank structure of labor. However, things have gone amuck due to the changing nature of work and the neoliberal emphasis on a globalized workforce. Rather than keeping jobs within the United States where union workers tirelessly struggled to obtain improved conditions of labor, capitalist have relocated or out-sourced production to "undeveloped" countries, where massive worker exploitation is carried out with greater ease and few environmental regulations or restrictions.

Meanwhile, the United States, keeping with its privileged status as economic leader of the world, has become the knowledge society. The consequence of this shift in the nature of work is the virtual disappearance of thousands of well-paying jobs, through rampant technological development and computerization—factors that although they might increase efficiency of capitalist interests also exacerbate the level of alienation and joblessness. Workers are increasingly functioning within virtual contexts that are now so commonsensical, that few even notice the ever-growing disconnection from the products of their labor. Moreover, the alienation provoked by this intense separation of workers and the natural world has reached such proportions that few seem to have the where-withal to halt its movement or to challenge the colonizing impact on our lives. Teachers too are implicated in this process as they are stripped of freedom to make decisions regarding curricula, while their pedagogical social agency is pacified with prepackaged materials, distance learning, and other technological devices linked to the control of teaching labor. For many, it just feels like an unstoppable "train of progress" on which one must board or be forever left in the obscurity of the past.

Even more disconcerting is the destructive impact that alienation and unbridled consumerism have had on working class students and their education. People, places, and things are all potential commodities, whose value is determined by the whims of the marketplace. Of this, Freire (1970b) argued, "Money is the measure of all things and profit the primary goal" (p. 44). Accordingly, the marketplace, through the process of fetishization, successfully "transforms everything surrounding it into an object of its domination. The earth, property, production, the creations of . . . [human beings]—everything is reduced to the status of objects" (p. 44). The process of fetishization is equally at work within schools, as it is in the society at large. Schools are constantly courted by large publishing companies hawking the latest educational textbooks and curricular materials that are deceptively "divorced from the leading ideas that shape and maintain them" (Macedo, 1994, p. 182). Companies, seeking to establish name recognition with young consumers, are eager to generously provide teachers with logo-ridden materials. Meanwhile, teachers, forced by necessity to spend hundreds of dollars on materials for their classroom without compensation, are only too happy to receive classroom resources, without regard for the corporate manipulation of young minds.

Freire argued that educational policies and practices have real economic consequences, particularly for working class students from racialized communities. In our work, we need to recognize that these consequences "are not just symbolic . . . they shape people's lives and their places in the material world" (Carnoy, 1987, p. 16), and nowhere is this more evident than in the arena of education. Through an unjust system of meritocracy, schools sort, select, and exclude students. Testing, assessment, and promotion policies determine which students are deemed worthy of opportunities and which are not. And just as there is nothing neutral about how the political economy is reproduced, there is nothing neutral about the manner in which these education practices promote racialized class formation.

A dual process of domestication and massification is also implicated in the narrow definition of success offered to working class students. Success is narrowly defined today as college entrance. Never mind that in the current neoliberal labor market, college graduates are greeted with shrinking job options. Never in the history of the United States have so many college graduates faced the prospects of underemployment or unemployment, after accumulating huge debt to attend university. Yet, despite these very real and concrete material conditions, schools continue to tout the college readiness mantra, without serious engagement with what is happening out in the world. Students, who defy, covertly or overtly, the limited choices handed them, find themselves generally ignored or eventually suspended or expelled, when teachers and school officials give up trying to "fix" their resistance and unwillingness to acquiesce to the hegemony of the college readiness code.

Freire (1983) viewed this limiting of student choices as entrenched within the capitalist mode of mass production—a culprit in the domestication and alienation of workers, their children, and their communities. Accordingly, he wrote:

Mass production as an organization of human labor is possibly one of the most potent instruments of [human] massification. By requiring a man [or woman] to behave mechanically, mass production domesticates him [or her]. By separating activity from the total project, requiring no total critical attitude toward production, it dehumanizes him [or her]. By excessively narrowing a man [or woman's] specialization, it constricts horizons, making him [or her] a passive fearful being . . . reducing critical capacity.

(p. 34)

Further, Freire connected this process of massification with the domestication of students' critical faculties, which fools them into believing they have choices. But the limited choices offered work well in the service of social containment, in that the majority of the population is actually excluded from the sphere where decisions are made by fewer and fewer people. Simultaneously, students and their parents are maneuvered to accept mythical explanations of reality that whittle their life choices. In turn, the process of education too is whittled down, as greater emphasis is placed on "training" programs founded on neoliberal pragmatism. On this point, Freire (1998a) was exceedingly clear: "Purely pragmatic training, with its implicit or openly expressed elitist authoritarianism, is incompatible with the learning and practice of becoming a 'subject'" (p. 46).

This phenomenon is particularly alarming at a time when the safety net of the welfare system has been effectively eroded by neoliberal polices of the last 30 years. In the process, the poorest people in the wealthiest country in the world are stripped of limited state resources available for their meager material existence. These conditions have intensified during the last decade, given that the great mortgage debacle of 2006 that heavily affected working class communities of color, leaving economists to predict that it will take another 25 years for our communities to recover from the collapse. Yet, in the midst of an increasing economic polarization, the meaning of democracy in this country remains synonymous with the freedom to consume. Seldom are students encouraged to critically interrogate what it means to be a free-market consumer or to consider the ecological downsides of overconsumption. Instead, capitalism has become the transcendent culture—a phenomenon that is achieved through the market's grip on the culture industry and its racialized manifestations. Through the hegemonic process, the marketplace homogenizes the dreams and desires of consumers, rendering cultural knowledges and indigenous wisdom inconsequential to the dictates of neoliberal rule.

Freire (1997) also expressed concern for the hidden curriculum of technology, which has become "a main bastion of capitalism" (p. 56). The global booming industry developed swiftly due to the enormously profitable connection it enjoyed with the burgeoning "information society," initiated in the late 20th century and the increasing move toward virtual education. Yet, seldom are important critical questions raised, given the zeal that schools express as they mount the technology bandwagon. In whose interest and to what purpose is technology functioning? When teachers increasingly insert technology into the process of classroom learning, what is the impact of technology on student relationships to one another and the natural world? By failing to critically engage these questions, Freire (1997) argued that much of the rhetoric on technology obscures that "technological advances enhance with greater efficiency the ideological support for material power" (p. 36). Freire, nevertheless, retained the dialectical tension in his argument, in that he did not consider the answer to be the rejection of the technology, but rather the process of our humanization. "I am a being who does not bow before the indisputable power accumulated by technology because, in knowing that it is a human production, I do not accept that it is, in and of itself, bad" (p. 35).

Deeply concerned with the contradictions inherent in the politics of the marketplace, Freire urged teachers to "detach ourselves from the idea that we are agents of capital" (McLaren, 2000, p. 191). Further, he argued that teachers must struggle "to retain a concept of the political beyond a reified consumer identity constructed from the panoply of market logic" (p. 152). Moreover, Freire (1998b) believed that educators

could support students from oppressed communities "to create a social, civic and political discipline which is absolutely
essential to the democracy that goes beyond bourgeois and
liberal democracy and that finally seeks to conquer the injustice and the irresponsibility of capitalism" (p. 89).

Freire (1997) asserted that the oppressive system of capitalist
production could not be altered without simultaneous collective
efforts to democratize schools and the larger society—which,
incidentally, is exactly what most reform strategies stifle, given
the logic of the marketplace and the quest for economic
supremacy that informs the politics of reformism. Not surprisingly, he urged instead "fighting against reformism" and
using "the contradictions of reformist practice to defeat it"
(p. 74). To help counter these contradictions, Freire urged us
to construct within schools and communities what he called
"advanced forms of social organizations ... capable of surpass-
ing this articulated chaos of corporate interests" (p. 36). This
again points to corporate policies of economic Darwinism
that promote deregulation, the free market, nationalism, and
militarism, through an ethnocentric ethos of "survival of the
fittest." The focus, in this instance, is confrontation with the
political economy of capitalism, which shamelessly justifies its
perilous impact upon millions of people and the destruction
of the Earth's ecosystem, by way of military supremacy and
international speculation.

We need only consult history to confirm that the politics
of colonization has been rooted in a violent project of economic exploitation and racialization, which has provided
the hegemonic apparatus to justify imperial expansionism
and unmerciful genocide and conquest of those deemed less
human. Returning to Freire's notion of capitalism as the root
of domination, it is useful in this analysis to also link past and

current colonizing forces to the subordinating role of a population's perceived capacity for productivity within capitalist society. This is to say that the basic worth of an individual or a people has been literally tied to their capacity to contribute to the process of capitalist accumulation. Hence, rather than pedagogical concern for our humanity, sovereignty, or the evolution of critical consciousness in the interest of culturally democratic life, banking educational objectives emphasize to what extent students have the potential to participate as consuming citizens of the empire.

Moreover, schools, as economic engines, function effectively in the process of class formation and the production of a national work force that is in sync with the requirements of the labor market and the military demands of a culture of perpetual war. It is here, where the politics of meritocracy in the United States, in conjunction with high-stakes testing, is effectively normalized and utilized to sort, sift, reward, or exclude students, accordingly. As would be expected, the children of the affluent rise to the top, while the majority of poor and working class students of color continue to populate the rosters of the academically underachieving—where they, their families, their culture, and their language are held suspect and responsible for their failure. All the while, the larger economic inequalities and hegemonic educational forces that negatively impact the lives of working class students remain veiled in a victim-blaming ideology of accountability and personal choice, along with the myth that equality and fair treatment is available to all deserving students who genuinely work hard. The unemployment crisis that has hit all sectors of the population in the last 5 years has begun to unveil this hypocrisy.

Coming to terms with the role of political economy in the process of schooling is essential to an emancipatory vision of schooling. Educators must not only come to accept responsibility for the power we hold within schools and communities, but also make wise decisions about how we use our power in the interest of constructing a practice that supports cultural and economic democracy. Freire contended that teachers who are unaware of the political nature of their power and authority will find themselves constantly falling into contradictions and unable to develop well-conceived alternative pedagogical approaches. This occurs most when educators lack coherent emancipatory principles from which to enact our teaching practice—outside the limiting culture of hegemony.

Betrayal of Multiculturalism

> To underestimate the wisdom that necessarily results from socio-cultural experience is at one and the same a scientific error, and the unequivocal expression of the presence of en elitist ideology.
>
> —Paulo Freire (2002)

In the early history of the civil rights movement, educators and activists of color viewed multicultural education as a counter-hegemonic alternative for decolonizing the curriculum and transforming classroom life. In the 1970s, notions of biculturalism—also tied to the struggle for bilingualism—began to evolve and efforts were forged toward developing culturally relevant pedagogies. Many of these pedagogical efforts were founded on the principles that Freire first outlined in *Pedagogy of the Oppressed*. Those principles challenged cultural invasion and the banking model of education and called for a problem posing pedagogy that would support the evolution of critical consciousness in the education of children from oppressed communities. Freire's notion of cultural invasion was overwhelmingly salient to those of us from communities with histories of genocide, slavery, and colonization.

However, as critical multicultural education efforts began to take hold in the late 1970s and early 1980s, reactionary conservative backlash and liberal rewriting of multiculturalism began to steadily erode the transformative intent and counterhegemonic purpose. Many of the multicultural education efforts that took hold in schools during the 1980s and 1990s, born of the burgeoning Neoliberal age, not only conserved a racializing hierarchical structure of power but also deficit notions, which served to readily sustain the meritocratic process of class formation within working class communities of color.

As communities of color employed the organizing potential of a politics of identity, in order to call for fundamental change to gross social and economic inequalities across the nation, the Reagan administration's *A Nation at Risk* report, issued in 1983, served as the perfect counter-revolutionary strategy to thwart our escalating movement for equality. With the veiled contention that schools should serve as economic engines to ensure the global superiority of the nation, the accountability movement began to gain steam. Neoliberal priorities of the state countered emancipatory agendas in every arena of social and economic policy, including education. The process of deregulation, privatization, and the erosion of the safety net resulted in an economic corporate boom in the decade that followed, while the burgeoning neoliberal agenda began to dismantle gains made by the civil rights movement. One disastrous impact to communities of color was the unprecedented increase in the number of U.S. incarcerations from 1984–2008, increasing from less than 500,000 inmates to over 2 million—with an overwhelming number of poor, working class inmates of color, 70% who were considered to be functionally illiterate.[2]

Rooted in a conservative ideology of deficit notions—whether of nature or nurture—"whitewashed" expectations of multicultural education became the norm, while discussions about the "race" problem or "race" as the determining factor in the academic underachievement of students of color prevailed in educational debates. In true colonizing and hegemonic style, many radical educators, particularly those of color, who remained aligned with Freire's pedagogical and political concerns, were pushed out and marginalized, as new "White" (liberal) multicultural education gurus descended on the stage to dominate and distort more revolutionary discourses born out of decolonizing struggles that had been waged by Black, Latino, Asian, and American Indian educators. In their place, well-meaning discourses of urgency, justified by liberal "cycle of poverty" interpretations—which blamed our children, families, and culture for our personal and community dysfunctions—were used as rationales for obstructing newly gained opportunities to evolve and advance our participation in decision making, even in the education of our children.

As a consequence, many of us found our innovative efforts warped into unrecognizable proportions, rationalizing once again the superiority of mainstream multicultural educators. Token educators of color who followed their lead were effectively integrated into schools and teacher preparation programs to marginalize more overt decolonizing discourses and practices of radical educators of color—a phenomenon whose consequence is being dramatically felt across the entire educational landscape today, as scholarship tied to cultural and language subordination in schools has gone out of vogue and now considered passé in the "flat world"[3] of neoliberal multiculturalism. In the process, the transformative potential of multicultural curriculum, text, and pedagogy has been all but stripped away, while a fragmented curriculum of cultural songs, stories, holidays, and heroes prevail, if at all.

With the eclipse of the so-called multicultural age in education, persisting problems and concerns raised by educators of color and their allies for almost a century, now fall on deaf ears, as the instrumentalizing ideology of neoliberal education has devised limiting matrices of accountability that deliberately discount historical and contemporary community concerns related to culture, language, class, pedagogy, power, and knowledge production. Instead, the numbers game of high-stakes testing, the standardization of knowledge, and teaching to the test are the order of the day. Consequently, we find ourselves today more deeply mired in Western ethnocentric notions of humanity, where individualism, object-based, future-focused, scientism, and materialism counteract the legitimacy of subordinate cultural community values and epistemological traditions of difference. Additionally, this leads to the negation of the worldviews of those deemed "other"—including the marginalization of communal strategies, ancestral knowledge, and spiritual traditions that might enhance the teaching and learning of our children. More often than not, well-meaning educators seeking to address the needs of working class communities of color continue to be entrapped in a deficit paradigm of difference.

Even more disconcerting is when critical educators of color, at all levels of education, attempt to challenge these deficit notions in our teaching and research. Mainstream educators, many who pride themselves in being social justice advocates or antiracist, greet us with resistance and unparalleled requests for legitimacy of claims, when we seek to express or enact our particular cultural paradigms and philosophical assumptions of humanity and community self-determination. These paradigms and assumptions that often reside outside many well-intended, but still colonizing, social values and epistemological priorities or directives, inadvertently objectify and render students from poor and working class communities of color passive agents of their own learning—in direct opposition to Freire's notion that students should reside at the center of their learning and that educators must begin with this as our starting point.

This, of course, echoes modernity's historical project of political and historical colonization, drafted from a conceptual narrative and societal design that legitimates and normalizes the economic and military domination, disempowerment, and dispossession of the majority of the world's population—in the name of democracy, progress, and profit. There is no question that the dehumanizing currents of the contemporary neoliberal agenda, which show trends of increasing inequalities in so-called developing countries, require us to grapple seriously with the struggle for our humanity, as Freire argued, in the face of hegemonic forces that seek to colonize every aspect of our lives, from birth to death. That is precisely why this issue is one that must remain central to any decolonizing epistemology, pedagogy, or methodology of classroom or community leadership.

The Cultural Context

> Respect for the knowledge of living experience is inserted into the
> larger horizon against which it is generated—the horizon of cultural

context, which cannot be understood apart from class particularities
. . . Respect for popular culture, then, implies respect for cultural
context.

—Paulo Freire (2002)

Central to Freire's (1983) pedagogical thesis of critical consciousness is an understanding of the significance of the cultural context in the process of knowledge production. Further,
he recognized culture as a collective human creation and "a
systematic acquisition of human experiences" (p. 49). This is
as true to the larger context of class formation as it is to the
question of bicultural formation where students must daily
navigate the tensions and power dynamics of the subordinate/
dominant divide. Hence, Freire's work has been and continues
to be fundamental to critical educators, educational leaders,
and activists of color, in that it reinforces the political necessity
of contextual knowledge. Culture is a systematic acquisition
of human experience (p. 48). This concept of culture links
decolonizing education to communal and ancestral knowledge, which neither transcends the individual subject nor the
material conditions that shape the histories and everyday relationships of formerly colonized and enslaved populations.

From this standpoint, if we are to contend, in theory and
practice, with the educational difficulties of students from
working class and racialized communities, we must look
beyond simply the personal or individual. We must seek
answers, as Freire argued, within the long histories of economic, social, and political of oppression, so that we might
better understand the forces and structures that give rise to
inequalities and social exclusion, as they currently exist within
our own lives and that of our students. Moreover, Freire's
writings also make an important case for the embodiment of

knowledge, which can potentially move us away from colonizing abstractions and separations of the body, a phenomenon that has always worked to the colonizing interest of the powerful and wealthy (Darder, 2011).

This to say, the underlying purpose of hegemonic power is to legitimate and conceal the imperial and colonial relations that today still undergird capitalism. As such, the political work of the oppressed has always required the unveiling, naming, and challenging of asymmetrical relations of power and their consequences within schools, communities, and the larger society. There is no question that Freire's pedagogy of the oppressed was articulated precisely with the intent to *speak truth to power* and, in so doing, create classroom conditions whereby student self-determination and critical consciousness could more readily flourish, in concert with educators committed to their critical formation.

It is from this political imperative that philosophical critiques related to objectivity, absolute knowledge, reductionism, ethnocentrism, and elitism, as well as structural critiques of class inequalities, cultural invasion, racism, sexism, heterosexism, and so on, have been waged. For some, this may echo the mantra of intersectionality, so often heard in oppositional discourses. However, as Rodolfo Torres and I (2004) have argued in *After Race: Racism After Multiculturalism*, intersectionality arguments still fail to confront the totalizing impact of capitalism. That is, racism, sexism, heterosexism, disablism, and all forms of oppression are deeply implicated in an interlocking set of relations that preserve and sustain the interests of capital and, therefore, do not function independently of an unjust distribution of wealth and power.

Beyond the obvious material dispossession of the impoverished working class, Freire spoke repeatedly about the manner in which conditions of economic exploitation and domination dehumanize our relationships, distorting our capacity to love one another, the world, and ourselves. In concert with Antonio Gramsci (1971) before him, Freire was well aware of how even well-meaning educators, through lack of politics or critical moral leadership, participate in disabling the hearts, minds, and bodies of students—an act that interferes with the development of the social agency and political comprehension required to engage and transform the debilitating social and material circumstances that betray our humanity.

Our Unfinishedness

> [Our] own unity and identity, in regards to others and the world, constitutes [our] essential and irrepeatable way of experiencing [ourselves] as cultural, historical, and unfinished beings in the world, simultaneously conscious of [our] unfinishedness . . . This unfinishedness is essential to our human condition. Wherever there is life, there is unfinishedness.
>
> —Paulo Freire (1998a)

Starting from the realization that we live in an unfree and unequal world, Freire affirmed that "our struggle for our humanization," had to evolve from our struggle for the emancipation of labor and the overcoming of our alienation,[4] so that we might affirm ourselves as full subjects of history. However, the pursuit of our full humanity, Freire (1970b) argued could not "be carried out in isolation or as individuals, but only in the fellowship and solidarity" (p. 85) of community and social movement. Thus, relationships of solidarity, built through collective labor, must remain central to our politics and our pedagogy, given that it is "in the process of revolution . . . that human beings in communion liberate each other" (p. 133). This understanding of social struggle as a collective undertaking has resonated deeply and powerfully with those who possess little power or influence over their lives, given the contradictions and constrictions at work in capitalist societies.

Freire often called to mind the significance of *unfinishedness* as an necessary radical variable in diminishing fatalism and inspiring hope in new possibilities for collective change among the oppressed. This recognition of human unfinished can also help unveil the hidden or silenced contradictions at work behind what Freire termed *limit situations*—contradictions that we must challenge and overcome in our efforts to reinvent schools and communities. At the heart of this concept of our humanity is also the recognition that oppression is never a permanent condition; and it is, indeed, because no human condition is ever absolute or finished that the struggle remains viable and hope fertile, even within political and material conditions that appear desolate and barren. Freire (1983) explained,

> If this world were a created finished world, it would no longer be susceptible to transformation. The human beings exists as such, and the world is a historical-cultural one, because the two come together as unfinished products in a permanent relationship, in which human beings transform the world and undergo the effects of their transformation. In this dynamic, historical-cultural process one generation encounters the objective reality marked out by another generation and receives through it the imprints of reality.
>
> (p. 147)

For Freire, our capacity to live free requires then a fundamental shift in the "imprints" by which leaders, educators, and students define our lives and the conditions of our labor. This requires moving beyond the internalization of our oppression, the ejection of colonizing ideologies of domination, toward the establishment of solidarity with others, the recognition of ourselves as subjects of history, the courage to speak out when necessary, and a well-developed sense of empowerment, in order that we might name, critique, decolonize, and reinvent our world anew, in the interest of a truly just and democratic future. In waging struggles for social change, Freire considered it an imperative that those who are oppressed come to believe and understand that domination does not exist within a closed world from which there is no exit. Instead, Freire (1970b) reminded us, "This struggle is possible only because dehumanization, although a concrete historical fact, is not a given destiny but the result of an unjust order that engenders violence . . . which in turn dehumanizes the oppressed" (p. 44).

Freire's writings acknowledged the psychological, physical, and spiritual violence that oppressed populations have endured for centuries at the hands of the powerful—a meaningful insight, given the ruthless physical and psychological violence so often experienced by communities of color. In today's neoliberal world, psychological violence in the guise of accountability is made palatable through veiled deficiency discourses of "high-risk" students, which Freire (1970b) likened to being "sweetened by false generosity, because it interferes with the [student's] ontological and historical vocation to be more fully human" (p. 55). He reasoned that situations of violence generally emerge out of subjugation and the negation of our humanity. About this, Freire wrote,

Violence is initiated by those who oppress, who exploit, who fail to recognize others as persons—not by those who are oppressed,

exploited, and unrecognized. It is not the unloved who initiate dis-
affection, but those who cannot love because they love only themselves. It is not the helpless, subject to terror, who initiate terror, but
the violent, who with their power create the concrete situation which
begets the "rejects of life." It is not the tyrannized who initiate des-
potism, but the tyrants. It is not the despised who initiate hatred, but
those who despise. It is not those whose humanity is denied them
who negate humankind, but those who denied that humanity (thus
negating their own as well).

(p. 55)

Freire, as Frantz Fanon before him, demonstrated political
fortitude and intellectual courage when he linked the question of violence to intentionality. His view on violence has
been particularly important to the struggle of the oppressed.
That is to say, that although Freire never condoned violence
in any of his speeches or writings, he clearly recognized that
there was a very different phenomenon at work in the violence engendered by those who seek to dominate and exploit
and the violence generated by the fight of those who seek to
counter their dehumanization. "And this fight, because of the
purpose given it by the oppressed, will actually constitute an
act of love, opposing the lovelessness which lies at the heart
of the oppressors' violence, lovelessness even when clothed in
false generosity" (1970b, p. 45).

Through his solid ontological fidelity to our unfinishedness,
Freire championed the possibilities of the oppressed to remake
history, through our commitment to struggle. For, it is precisely because oppression exists as an impermanent, incom-
plete, and changing historical phenomenon—constructed
by human beings—that we as decolonized and empowered
subjects of history possess the possibility of transforming its

configuration. Our task then as critical educators committed to a just world is to embrace fully this dialectical understanding of our relationship with the world, so that together we might transform our teaching and learning into a revolutionary praxis—a critical praxis that encompasses reflection, dialogue, and action, where theory and practice are regenerating and in alliance (Darder, 2002).

Freire (1997) knew that this way of life requires a critical commitment to move beyond piety, sentimentalism, and individualistic gestures, so that we might "risk an act of love" and enter into sustaining and nurturing political relationships of dialogue and solidarity—communal relationships grounded upon our unwavering fidelity to break out of the domesticating and colonizing conditions that trick us into complicity with "an economy that is incapable of developing programs according to human needs and that coexists indifferently to the hunger of millions to whom everything is denied" (p. 36).

In *Teachers as Cultural Workers,* Freire (1998b) acknowledged that radical struggles, by those who dare to exercise their political will and capacity within schools, could be severely curtailed by the tendency to become "hardened" by the dominant bureaucracy's oppressive expectations and dehumanizing posture toward those who critique the system and work toward social change. He recognized that, more often than not, this phenomenon is prevalent because critical educators—particularly educators of color—committed to a Freirian inspired pedagogy of freedom are perceived by institutional gatekeepers as disruptive and destructive, while our efforts to achieve greater freedom and autonomy are discouraged or punished, even by those who would call themselves our allies. In efforts to control and "inanimate" teachers and students of color, conservative educational bureaucracies and policies of schooling often "deter the drive to search, that restlessness and creativity that characterizes life" (Freire, 1970b, p. 46). In response, Freire argued that genuine forms of learning must aim critically to unveil the contradictions and courageously challenge practices that objectify, dispirit, and dehumanize, preventing our political expression as full cultural citizens. Educational oppression, in the flesh, consists of policies and practices of social control, by which teachers, students, and parents from historically oppressed communities are permitted, for the most part, only enough opportunity to fulfill roles prescribed by their social class.

Freire recognized and often spoke of the enormity and difficulty of the pedagogical vision that he proposed. Nevertheless, he could see no alternative for the restoration of our humanity than to eradicate the debilitating fatalism and imposed myths, which seek to alienate and render us passive, while underhandedly seeking our consensus and participation in our own oppression. Often, this is accomplished through bourgeois notions of morality that function to reinforce our disempowerment, bringing to mind the words by former Black Panther, Assata Shakur, who argued, "Nobody in the world, nobody in history, has ever gotten their freedom by appealing to the moral sense of the people who were oppressing them."[5] Hence, Freire (1970b) repeatedly asserted that no one can empower the oppressed, but rather it is the oppressed who must empower themselves, if true emancipation is to prevail. That said, the role of the privileged ally is to use their privilege to create the conditions by which the disenfranchised can truly "become beings for themselves" (p. 74).

This political project of emancipation, however, requires our sustained collective labor—a labor born of love, but deeply anchored in an unceasing political commitment to know, through both theory and practice, the nature of the beast that preys upon our humanity; and with this knowledge, fight with unwavering hope and solidarity. For many of us from poor and working class communities of color, the option of struggle was never a choice, but rather a political necessity, if we were to empower ourselves and ensure our right to exist in sync with the cultural wisdom forged from our own lived histories of survival as tribes, nations, and peoples.

Indeed, Freire's revolutionary vision points to the need for an ongoing political process of personal and community struggle that demands ongoing critical vigilance. This demands a willingness to courageously and consistently persist in a process of personal and collective reflection, regarding the consequences of our theory and action. For Freire (1983), this is an essential component of our pedagogy and politics, for as educators are placed "face to face before themselves they investigate and question themselves" (p. 150), enlivening their practice. This intimate engagement of self underscores the revolutionary accountability that educators and leaders must enact in efforts to transform conditions of inequality. Through a sustained process of personal and political accountability, we can labor in schools and communities with greater coherence, humility, and love.

Notes

1 Cited in Facundo, B. *How Is Freire Seen in the United States?* Facundo's article here sets down a rather scathing critique of Freire that simply does not coincide with my experience of Freire's work in communities of color. Nevertheless, I respect her efforts here. See www.bmartin.cc/dissent/documents/Facundo/section2.html

2 See, *The Punishing Decade: Prison and Jail Estimates at the Millennium.* [1] May 2000. Justice Policy Institute; Historical Corrections Statistics in the United States, 1850–1984. NCJ 102529. Published in 1986; Correctional

Population Trends Chart. U.S. Bureau of Justice Statistics. Number of prison and jail inmates from 1980 onwards; and *Sourcebook of Criminal Justice Statistics* (uses BJS data).

3 The reference here is to Thomas L. Friedman's *The World Is Flat,* a book that glorifies the accomplishments of a globalized neoliberalism but fails to engage the realities of an increasingly unequal world. What Friedman means by "flat" is "connected": the lowering of trade and political barriers and the exponential technical advances of the digital revolution, which have made it possible to do business, or almost anything else, instantaneously with billions of other people across the planet. Again, the question is who exactly can do business or anything else?

4 Freire, P. (1970b) op.cit. (28).

5 Shakur, Assata. *The People Record.* See, http://thepeoplesrecord.com/post/31671382262/nobody-in-the-world-nobody-in-history-has-ever

2

PEDAGOGY OF LOVE: EMBODYING OUR HUMANITY

I think that it could be said when I am no longer in this world: "Paulo Freire was a man who lived. He could not understand life and human existence without love and without the search for knowledge . . . "

—Paulo Freire (1993)

Paulo Freire's view on the significance of love to both our pedagogical and political lives remains steadfast and resounding across the landscape of his writings. Freire believed deeply—from the personal to the pedagogical to the political—in the transformative and emancipatory power of love. Freire's radical articulation of love spoke to both a personal and political Eros, grounded in an unwavering faith in the oppressed to generate the political will necessary to transform our lives and the world. In Freire's eyes, to attempt daily engagement with societal forces that dehumanize and undermine our existence, without the power of love on our side, was like lost sojourners walking in a vast desert, with insufficient water to complete the crossing. Hence, it is not surprising that Freire (1998b) often came back to the notion of an "armed loved—the fighting love of those convinced of the right and the duty to fight, to denounce, and to announce" (p. 42). His is a concept of love not only meant to comfort or assuage the suffering of the oppressed, but also to awaken within us the historical thirst for justice and the political wherewithal to reinvent out world.

Freire's love permeated his existence as a man and an educator. He could be gentle, tender, and inspiring, while at the same time, critical, challenging, and strategic in unveiling individual or collective follies. As such, Freire's pedagogy of love challenged deeply the false generosity of those whose ideologies and practices work to sustain a system of education that transgresses at its very core every emancipatory principle of social justice and democratic life. It was Freire's lucid understanding of love as an untapped political force of consciousness that most drew me to his work and today continues to fuel my commitment to the emancipatory political project he championed throughout his life.

In my academic preparation, never had another educational theorist so fearlessly given the question of love such primacy in his philosophy, pedagogy, or politics. Moreover, he did this *de corazón* (from the heart), without concern for the consequences of mean-spirited critiques that cast him as unsystematic or unscientific. For a student whose life was mired by the lovelessness of oppression, Freire's (1970b) commitment to "the creation of a world in which it will be easier to love" spoke to the suffering of my heart, the weariness of my spirit, and the yearning of my soul. Hence, it is not surprising that I would turn here to Freire's pedagogy of love as a political force–a philosophy that fundamentally inspired my political and intellectual formation as a critical scholar.

Love as a Political Force

> I have a right to love and to express my love to the world and to use it as a motivational foundation for struggle.
>
> —Paulo Freire (1998a)

Understanding *love as a political force* is essential to understanding Freire's revolutionary vision of consciousness and transformation. The inseparability with which he theorized the political significance of love in the evolution of consciousness and political empowerment is key to our ability to grasp accurately the depth of Freire's meaning. In keeping with Eric Fromm's (1956, 1964) contribution to this question, expressed so formidably in his book *The Art of Loving,* Freire did not see love as a mere sentimental exchange between people, but rather love constitutes an intentional spiritual act of consciousness that emerges and matures through our social and material practices, as we work to live, learn, and labor together. Across Freire's books is found this critical view of love, often glossed over by the very people who most need to comprehend deeply his humanizing intent. Sometimes more directly and other times more subtly, Freire reminded us that a politics of love must serve as the underlying force of any political project that requires us to counter daily with oppression, as we simultaneously seek in its midst new possibilities for transformation.

Freire wrote of the politics of love by engaging with the personal and communal exchanges he considered important to the relationship between teachers and students. In particular, he sought to promote the importance of cultivating greater intimacy between self, others, and the world, in the process of our teaching and learning. Freire (1997) believed that "living with [democracy] and deepening it so it has real meaning in people's everyday lives" (Carnoy, 1987, p. 12) should be a significant political concern of an emancipatory classroom. Here, democracy and the solidarity necessary for its evolution are made possible through a pedagogy fortified by the universal regard for the dignity and equality of all people, no matter their differences or circumstances. Freire's view of love as a dialectical force that simultaneously unites and respects difference, must be imagined as a radical sense of lived kinship, if we are to effectively transform the social and material conditions of inequality and disaffiliation that are the hallmark of capitalism. Freire speaks to a love generated from political grace and born of collective consciousness that emerges from our shared curiosity, creativity, and imagination, giving meaning to both our resistance and counterhegemonic practice.

Through a commitment to love and labor together for a more just world, Freire sincerely believed that relationships of solidarity can be nurtured and political dreams of freedom regenerated. Freire often asserted the notion that we, as human beings, must unite ourselves with the world and others in the process of social and political cocreation—so that our shared participation in the labor of struggle could impel us toward a deeper sense of ourselves as historical beings. This is also a force that moves us beyond spiritual transcendence, personal-abnegation, or political negations of the dialectic between consciousness and the material. Rather, Freire asserted a love that is born and emerges directly out of our social participation and unwavering political commitment to the transformation of that historical moment in which we exist as grounded subjects.

Keeping all this in mind, we can better appreciate Freire's concern with the dehumanizing forces so prevalent in hegemonic schooling. He was adamant about the political necessity to unveil authoritarian pedagogies in the classroom, which curtail the pleasure of life and the principle of love, generating in both teachers and students a sense of alienation and estrangement from self and the world. This, in turn, arouses deep anxieties and insecurities that interfere with cultivating and nurturing the political imagination, epistemological curiosity, and the joy of learning necessary to our practice. Freire (1970a) wrote in *Pedagogy of the Oppressed* about this historical and systematic disregard for the respect and dignity of students that serves, on one hand, to breed helplessness and disempowerment; while, on the other, it spawns uncritical forms of resistance that can work against the interests of the oppressed. Freire contended that oppression is best served by keeping the oppressed confused and estranged from one another, steeped in sentiments of fatalism and inferiority that blame students for their academic failure and workers for their material misfortunes.

In his conceptualization of love as a motivational force for struggle, Freire linked his pedagogy of love to political values that nurture emancipatory relationships. Some of these include faith and dignity in our relationships with others, social responsibility for our world, participation in the coconstruction of knowledge, and solidarity across our differences. Directly and indirectly, Freire touched on the essence of love as inseparable to our labor as educators and democratic citizens of the world. Again, true to Fromm's (1964) adage, Freire embraced the idea that "[o]ne loves that for which one labors, and one labors for that which one loves" (p. 26). This points undeniably to the extent to which Freire, himself, intimately and passionately loved the world—a significant feature of both his pedagogy and personal way of being, whether with children, students, colleagues, family, friends, or simply the many people who crossed his path each day.

Although there are those who summarily issue feminist critiques of Freire's ideas and language to diminish the power of its political influence, it is ironically nearly impossible—true to feminist sensibilities—to separate the political and the personal when engaging Freire's work. Throughout his life, Freire resisted such separation in his own philosophy, political interpretations, and pedagogical praxis. Grounded in an enormous sense of responsibility to use his privilege in the interest of the oppressed, Freire stressed the importance of practicing respect, patience, and faith, if we are to dismantle the structures of domination that alienate and exploit those who exist, overwhelmingly, as slaves of capital, no matter our illusions.

In the process of teaching and learning, it is impossible to express love and respect for students without our willingness to engage them in ways that allow us to know them authentically. This is a form of knowing that demands we transcend our self-absorption and authoritarian fixations, in ways that open us horizontally to know and be known. In many respects, Freire's own capacity for love was an exercise in precisely this humanizing relational dynamic—one that seeks to identify or empathize with the core of another, beyond simply superficial responses or stereotypical distortions. For example, often working class students of color are perceived as being angry; but rather than to see them beyond preconceptions of anger or to acknowledge that all human beings who are anxious, worried, isolated, fearful, repressed, or suffering can exhibit moments of anger, most often teachers stop at the surface of the anger and, from there, issue racialized characterizations, devoid of insight into conditions that might inform students of color to express anger or frustration. And, even more disconcerting, seldom do teachers confront their own distortions that cause them to respond defensively and more authoritarian in their response to working class students of color.

Given the manner in which racialized accusations of anger have been so often used to exclude and undermine the voices of teachers, students, parents, and communities of color, it is useful to take a moment here to note that, according to Freire (1998a), "the kind of education that does not recognize the right to express appropriate anger against injustice, against disloyalty, against the negation of love, against exploitation, and against violence fails to see the educational role implicit in the expression of these feelings" (p. 45). He often noted that the right to be angry, just as the right to love, serves as a legitimate motivational foundation for our liberatory struggles; in that just anger can remind us that we are not supposed to live as objects of oppression. In the same light, Freire (1998a) insisted,

> my right to be angry presupposes that the historical experience in which I participate tomorrow is not a given, but a challenge and a problem. My just anger is grounded in any indignation in the face of the denial of the right inherent in the very essence of the human condition.
>
> (p. 71)

Therefore, one of the most important tasks of a pedagogy of love is to create the conditions for students to "engage in the experience of assuming themselves as social, historical, thinking, communicating, transformative, creative persons; dreamers of possible utopias, capable of being angry because of a capacity to love" (p. 45).

This is particularly so, given that many educators are so disconnected from the conditions of "the other" and frightened by their racialized misconceptions to allow themselves to genuinely know their students as vital human beings. Instead, students remain objects to be managed, manipulated, and controlled, in ways that may eventually draw out of them the prescribed answers. As a consequence, the classroom becomes routinized by standards of disembodied expectations removed from the organic responses of student bodies, while teachers conduct themselves "professionally" in ways that distance them from the possibility of expressing authentic human love— beyond the often cliché: "I love all my students!"

However, since students are not objects or static products to be tweaked here and there, Freire knew that learning, like loving, is an act that students must choose freely to practice, through the exercise of their social agency and personal empowerment. With this at the core of his pedagogical sensibilities, Freire also argued that teachers had to avert fixed notions or prescriptions of "the other," for given the changing and evolving nature of our humanity, seldom can we know our students or even ourselves fully. At best, we can usually know one another only in context and in relation to our shared labor or lived experiences. In fact, it is precisely this unpredictable and dynamic aspect of our humanity that most provides us that rich terrain for cultivating transformative consciousness, in ways that nurture our human complexities and respond to our yearning for freedom.

In his work, P. Freire (1995) spoke of love for his students, but always in relation to teaching. "When I say to love I mean to love the very process of teaching." (p. 20). In this process of teaching, he reasoned that the forces of love, beauty, and ethics converge to facilitate and enhance a communal experience of learning. Hence, Freire understood his love for students *within* this process of teaching. Of this he wrote,

> It is impossible to think of separating beauty from teaching; beauty from ethics; and the love for students from loving the process through which I must love the student. I love my students not because they are in a room where I am teacher. I love my students to the extent in which I love the very process of being with them.
>
> (p. 20)

In contrast, the banking model of education, with its objectification of students as static vessels to be filled with knowledge, thwarts the establishment of an emancipatory process of learning and, thus, constitutes an act of disrespect and violence. Consequently, this lovelessness undermines our human capacity for solidarity and erodes away the beauty of teaching and learning together, across our differences.

Solidarity and Difference

> Our fight against the different discriminations, against any negation of our being, will only lead to victory if we can realize the obvious: unity within diversity.
>
> —Paulo Freire (1997)

Freire argued that the relationship between teaching and loving is fundamental to our pedagogical and political potential, in that only through our courage to love, in the face of difference, is solidarity even a possibility—a solidarity that opens us to know and experience one another, both individually and collectively, within shared moments of tenderness, intellectual uncertainties, doubts, breakthroughs of knowledge, or social anxieties linked to repressed human suffering. In this way, solidarity and difference intertwine to create the social and material space for students to critique oppressive attitudes and practices of their everyday. In an emancipatory classroom, where a shared sense of community prevails, students' critical engagement with the conflicts and contradictions of difference work to sustain the development of critical social consciousness and, thus, bring about conditions that change us all.

Although many educators from subordinate communities dislike the term *tolerance,* P. Freire (1995) cast a critical view of tolerance as an important political virtue that is difficult to enact, in that, more often than not, the tolerance-intolerance dialectic is shut down. He explained tolerance as that quality which requires we move outside ourselves,

> It is the ability to enjoy difference. It is to learn from the difference. It means not to consider ourselves better than others precisely because they are different from us. When we think about tolerance we immediately think about racism which is the strongest negation of being tolerant; the lowest level of the negation of differences.
>
> (p. 21)

In contrast, intolerance thwarts the political rights of oppressed population to choice and the freedom to be. Furthermore, Freire's critical reading of tolerance does not degenerate into forms of indifference or irresponsibility. Rather, underlying this view is the belief that *love is tolerant.* Herein lies the transformative potential of a genuine solidarity—one not rooted in the negation of difference, but rather in a meaningful reinvention of classroom life and society; where love as a driving pedagogical force consummates the construction of knowledge, through the power of student dialogues founded upon their lived histories. About this relationship between dialogue and love, Freire wrote (1970b),

> Dialogue cannot exist . . . in the absence of a profound love for the world and for people. The naming of the world, which is an act of creation and re-creation, is not possible if it is not infused with love. Love is at the same time the foundation of dialogue and dialogue itself . . . Because love is an act of courage, not of fear, love is commitment to others . . . If I do not love the world—if I do not love life—if I do not love people—I cannot enter into dialogue.
>
> (pp. 90–91)

It is also within everyday expressions of solidarity and difference that teachers and students come to embrace the powerful dialectic of teacher-student and student-teacher, at the heart of Freire's pedagogy. Through the tension inherent in this process, teachers and students learn to construct knowledge together, discovering a powerful sense of oneness amidst difference and difference even at the core of oneness. For without cultivating this level of shared openness, humility, and compassion (beyond the dictates of the ego), classroom knowledge becomes an object to manipulate and possess, rendering it quickly stagnant, fragmented, and lifeless.

In turn, teachers and students can experience isolation and disconnection, in a perpetual game of sordid competition that offers but fleeting moments of satisfaction within a stagnant consciousness of domination. The utilitarian and individualistic nature of capitalist relations systematically functions within the classroom and the workplace to thwart cultural kinships, communal affiliations, and even familial loyalties, which potentiate the development and deepening of intimacy and solidarity. In the process, students and workers alike become more and more estranged from one another, their labor, and the world around them. In the process, reactionary humanist calls for community—whether defined by neighborhood, religion, "race," nationality, or class—often emerge in the hopes of overcoming a deepening sense of isolation and social abandonment.

For Freire, the enactment of radical love in the classroom, in contrast, seeks to build a democratic field of critical praxis, in which numbing experiences of alienation can be openly named, challenged, and dismantled, creating a place for teachers and students to contend more honestly and effectively with the human differences that exist between us, as we discard reactionary tendencies. This also entails a dialectical acknowledgment that "there is a constant oscillation in the rise and fall of discrimination: one should neither believe in guaranteed progress nor become fatalist about it."[1]

Cultural differences in the classroom are also worthy of discussion here, in that Freire, again, urges us to hold steady within the dialectical tension of differences—differences that can either stimulate greater curiosity, imagination, and questioning or cause dissonance, frustration, and anger, when students are not provided substantive opportunities for expression or guidance about the wisdom their cultural knowledge offers to the practice of democratic life. Unfortunately, too often hegemonic practices of schooling disrupt processes of democratic awakening, narrowing the field for aliveness, open-mindedness, and solidarity. Accordingly, hegemonic classroom environments deter the expression of decolonizing forms of knowledge, which are derived, more often than not, from the excluded cultural and linguistic sensibilities of students' lived histories and experiences.

It should not be surprising then to discover that one of the greatest challenges that teachers face in our efforts to embody a pedagogy of love is the establishment of cultural and linguistic democracy in the classroom. This is akin to Freire's notion of unity-in-diversity, which is also at the heart of his theorizing about the ethics of difference and democratic life. Fundamental to this concept is the recognition that the process of liberation, whether in the classroom or the larger society, can only be enacted through a political vision where neither unity nor difference is sacrificed. This is particularly noteworthy, in that ostensibly democratic societies tend to exhibit an overwhelming degree of homogeneity and conformity, instilled by banking education. This concept extends onto the realm of the economy in countries like the United States, where gross economic disparities are the norm and social mobility, contrary to commonsensical claims, belies the mantra that education ensures personal economic gain.

Of course, the unacknowledged conformity of the classroom and the economy are perpetuated by way of contradictory hegemonic structures and social mechanisms that condition students to think of themselves as solely individual possessors and consumers, with little regard for the common good or sense of responsibility for our communal existence. In conjunction, Freire (1970b) spoke to this tendency of capitalism to commodify.

> In their unrestrained eagerness to possess, the oppressors develop the conviction that it is possible for them to transform everything into objects of their purchasing power; hence their strictly materialistic concept of existence. Money is the measure of all things, and

profit the primary goal. For the oppressors, what is worthwhile is to have more—always more—even at the cost of the oppressed having less or having nothing. For them, *to be is to have* and to be the class of the "haves."

(p. 58, emphasis in original)

This possessing consciousness is often reinforced through advertising slogans and differentiating paraphernalia of the marketplace that readily assure consumers that they are, indeed, not only all different, but special. This distorting market ideology is embedded in the hidden curriculum of education and the meritocratic culture of elitism and privilege that prevails within schools and the larger social sphere.

This assimilative inclination of the classroom generally remains unaddressed, so that decolonizing forms of knowledge simply cannot surface, in this closed field of banking education. Further, the manufacturing of the insidious belief in the "uniqueness of each individual" by the culture industry functions effectively not only to thwart genuine epistemologies of differences, but also supports policies and practices of what Freire (1970b) called *cultural invasion*. Here he referred to

relationships between the invader and invaded [that] are situated at opposite poles. They are relationships of authority. The invader acts, the invaded are under the illusion that they are acting through the action of the other; the invader has his say, the invaded, who are forbidden this, listen to what the invader says.

(p. 17)

This relationship continues as an overarching condition even in schools where communities of color desire for their children to experience greater connection with their cultural traditions, primary languages, and histories of survival. The political consequence of hegemonic schooling is the wholesale denial or erasure of communal histories, cultural knowledge, and political self-determination—often replaced with superficial multicultural interventions that do little to respect the dignity or human rights of students, whose histories are indelibly marked by centuries of genocide, slavery, colonization, and economic exploitation.

The increasing tendency to eliminate differences within schools and society is in sync with the hegemonic apparatus of capitalist schooling that once openly drove the Americanization movement in the United States and persists in homogenized contortions of neoliberal multiculturalism—where cultural recognition on the surface belies the absence of power. As such, the new politics of assimilation is tied to deceptive notions of "equality" and "fairness," which seem oblivious to the gross accelerating inequality in the distribution of wealth and power—a phenomenon antagonistic to pedagogical expressions of radical love or democratic life. Thus, "in contemporary capitalistic society the meaning of equality now refers to the equality of automatons—human beings who in fact are devoid of their individuality" (Fromm, 1964, p. 15). This, in part, is linked to the alienating culture of capitalism, which results in the suppression of cultural differences, on the one hand, and the production of social exclusions, on the other. This phenomenon is well-oriented toward also instilling a false sense of national unity, informed by an entrenched and pervasive culture of U.S. consumerism and militarism.

Commonsense notions of equality and difference in capitalist society function well to persuade consumers into believing that they are, indeed, individuals, while simultaneously they adhere collectively to the dictates of the marketplace.

In this way, mass forms of standardization can prevail, while most members of society steeped in the ethers of their "individual uniqueness," seem indifferent. Hence, it is no wonder that there are not more protests and demonstrations waged against wealth inequality or high-stakes testing or the current national standardization of the curriculum, which seems to have received little objection, beyond the cost of implementation. In the name of conformity, the construction of knowledge, movement of the body, expression of human feeling, and even the practice of spirituality are miserably routinized and violently hijacked within traditional classrooms or community institutions charged with the social and political task of public containment of the masses.

In direct opposition, Freire affirmed the revolutionary power of love to enliven our teaching and create the conditions whereby our students experience the meaning and practice of living democracy. Educational practices powered by radical love also create the conditions where students can critically explore their cultural histories, which can also enhance their individual expression within the classroom. The power behind this pedagogical approach is that it simultaneously breaks barriers that isolate and objectify students, while supporting them to integrate into the heart of classroom life.

The democratizing aspirations of a pedagogy of love are, indeed, far easier to describe on these pages than to practice consistently. This is particularly so, in that it requires teachers to risk vulnerability, when forging democratic relationships with their students, even in the midst of external political struggles that may place pedagogical and curricular constraints upon them. Hence, Freire (1970b) considered the practice of revolutionary love in the classroom to constitute *an act of courage and risk,* in that this practice must also be linked to a larger humanizing ethos of education.

Toward a Humanizing Education

> To surmount the situation of oppression, people must first critically recognize its causes, so that through transforming action they can create a new situation, one which makes possible the pursuit of a fuller humanity.
>
> —Paulo Freire (1970b)

A pedagogy of love can best be understood as a deeply purposeful educational practice, fueled by an emancipatory political vision rooted in what Freire (1970b) considered our "true vocation: to be human." Underlying Freire's perspective is a political commitment to a larger humanizing political project of schools and society. This critical conceptualization of humanity encompasses a deeply reflective understanding and political interpretation of the dialectical relationship that exists between our cultural existence as individuals and our political and economic existence as communal beings. Accordingly, Freire understood capitalism as a system of production that denies the humanity of workers, encouraging the wholesale accumulation of material wealth by the few, with little concern for the suffering of those exploited and disempowered in the process. This dynamic is replicated across society, including the policies and practices that inform schools, whether public, charter, or private.

Hence, if educators are to effectively engage the difficulties that students from oppressed communities face, then, this requires that we move beyond solely an individualistic or psychologized understanding of our students and embrace them as both political and communal human beings with enormous potential for not only achieving academically but also with innate potential to transform the concrete conditions that erode their well-being. This requires that we seek answers within the historical realm of economic, social, and political forms, so that we might better understand the structures and political forces that give rise to our humanity, as it currently exists. Accordingly, a humanizing vision of pedagogy nurtures critical consciousness and social agency, in ways that move students away from instrumentalized forms of learning and replaces these with pedagogical activities that ignite both their passion for learning and their creative engagement with the world around them.

The same rich humanizing quality that Freire brought to his writings was also profoundly apparent in his love for life, freedom, and learning; as well as the ways he sought to share the transformative power of this love in his praxis—whether in a small group or a large auditorium of people. Freire consistently expressed a deep sense of joy and love for life, no matter how difficult the conditions or circumstances he had to confront, as an individual or in struggle with others. Again, the political and personal comingle fully here, in that Freire's commitment was consistently expressed as both a personal struggle to be free and a collective struggle for the emancipation of our collective humanity. Similarly, he urged educators to embrace our labor in schools and communities with love and respect for our students, as creators of their own lives and cocreators of the new world to come.

Freire recognized the nature of human beings beyond simply cognitive or mental beings. The sense that we are integral beings encompasses an understanding of our humanity as the combination of our physical, emotional, and spiritual faculties, in addition to the cognitive. Freire cultivated through his world a pedagogy that asks teachers to examine the world beyond the surface of what we often term reality. Instead, He posited a problem-posing approach, anchored in dialogue and a radical principle of love, by which teachers and students can come to critically know ourselves and the world. Within this pedagogical practice, Freire sought to contend openly and consistently with the manner in which oppression dehumanizes teachers and students alike. Freire was concerned with the manner in which even well-meaning teachers, through a lack of critical moral leadership, can participate in disabling the heart, minds, and bodies of students—an act that alienates students, forecloses their self-determination, and undermines their political formation. Instead, through a pedagogy that deliberately supports the awakening of critical consciousness, Freire sought to shatter rigid prescriptions of the oppressed and to fight for the restoration of our humanity.

Although some critiqued Freire's ideas as unrealistic or impossible to enact, these critiques are unwarranted. Never did Freire believe that an emancipatory pedagogy or political struggle could magically or instantly transform our consciousness or the world. Instead, he consistently pointed to the hard work required to bring forth any profound change to our lives, the schools in which we teach, and the communities in which we live and labor. What Freire did believe was that through dialogue and relationships of struggle, we could begin to summon the human power and material conditions necessary to reinvent the world around us. He insisted that we could do this through creating new language and new forms of being, which spoke genuinely to democratic possibilities and our existential yearning for freedom. Related to this difficult process, Freire also often warned us of the difficulties we must be prepared to face, in that often at the very moment when structural change is palpable, reactionary backlash can arise, rooted in an extreme and uncompromising negation of democratic possibilities. In direct contrast, Freire's pedagogy of love diametrically opposed such a negation of our humanity, working instead to create the emancipatory conditions necessary for social empowerment through a critical praxis of the body.

The Indispensability of the Body

> It is the human body, young or old, fat or thin, of whatever color, the conscious body that looks at the stars. It is the body that writes. It is the body that speaks. It is the body that fights. It is the body that loves and hates. It is the body that suffers. It is the body that dies. It is the body that lives!
>
> —Paulo Freire (in Freire & Faundez, 1989)

Freire left behind a legacy that speaks passionately to the relationship between love, the body, and knowledge. This encompasses a pedagogical perspective that is fully cognizant about the power of both the discipline of love and the primacy of the body in the construction of knowledge. Freire's pedagogy of love is anchored to an understanding that we are material beings and that the idea of loving, in the pedagogical sense, entails a humanizing ethos of classroom life that supports dialogue and solidarity, as we labor for the common good. As teachers and students participate more fully in the dialogical process of communal learning, the materiality of their bodies also become rightful allies in the formation and expression of collective consciousness. Of this Freire (1983) said, "true education incarnates the permanent search of people together with others for their becoming fully human in the world in which they exist" (p. 96).

Embracing the rightful place of the body in the classroom requires a view of students as integral human beings. It is this integral view that is negated within banking education, where a more complex understanding of the body and its significance to students' intellectual and political formation are absent. Since the epistemological focus is on analytical processes, other important ways of knowing are easily ignored or dismissed. As a result, student voices and other physical expressions of the body that fall outside the mainstream register are systematically silenced or shut down. It is also worth noting that this phenomenon is predicated upon a dominant notion of the individual as a psychological self, whose intelligence and "ego strength" are supposedly gauged by the ability to function, irrespective of external conditions.

As a consequence, educators prepared in the Western paradigm of self seldom possess the political acumen necessary to deflect deficit notions, so that they can engage critically with the larger social inequalities that shape the lives of historically oppressed populations. Accordingly, educators often are taught to place a great deal of attention upon classroom management and control of transgressive expressions of the body seen as disrupting to the pseudo-harmony of the classroom. Common authoritarian responses to student physicality ignore the meaning and intent behind student behavior, converting the body into an object that must acquiesce to the teacher's will or be expelled. In the process, little attention is given to the dialectical relationship that students have with their world—a relationship that for working class students of color requires constant navigation of the minefields of structural oppression perpetuated by racism, poverty, and other forms of social exclusions.

The material conditions and histories of our students are made visible on their bodies. Their histories of survival are witnessed in their skin, their teeth, their hair, their gestures, their speech, and the movement of their arms and legs. As such, bodies are "maps of power and identity" (Haraway, 1990, p. 2) that provide meaningful information and powerful insights into the tensions, struggles, and needs that students from oppressed communities express in the classroom. Freire (1998a) concluded, therefore, that it is insufficient to rely on abstract approaches to learning, where disembodied words and texts are privileged in the construction of knowledge. He argued, "words not given body (made flesh) have little or no value" (p. 39) to the process of liberation. His concern here was with the manner in which educational processes of estrangement causes a false dichotomy that alienate students from their world—the only true realm from which liberatory education can emerge.

This requires that teachers and students labor in the flesh. This is to say that our practices of teaching and learning be rooted in the materiality of human existence, as a starting place for critical praxis. Freire (1993) argued that

> [w]e learn things about the world by acting and changing the world around us. It is [through] this process of change, of transforming the material world from which we emerged, [where] creation of the cultural and historical world takes place. This transformation of the world [is] done by us while it makes and remakes us.
>
> (p. 108)

However, he was also clear that there is nothing automatic or natural about this process of social change nor is it a process that can solely rely on calculating logic or cold rationality. Moreover, given the body's sentient quality that overwhelmingly shapes student experiences and responses to the world, just or unjust, their bodies will constantly resist or desist, adjust or rebel, rejoice or despair, in the long human quest to be free.

The human body, further, constitutes a significant political terrain from which all emancipatory knowledge must emerge. Without the materiality of the body, our teaching and learning is reduced to a process of abstraction and fragmentation that attempts to falsely render knowledge a neutral and objective phenomenon, absent of history and ideology. Freire recognized that it is the body that provides us the medium for our existence as subjects of history and as politically empowered agents of change. Within the context of gross inequalities, this is particularly salient in that "bodies are also the primary means by which capitalism does its job (McLaren, 1998, p. xiii). We are molded and shaped by the structures, policies and practices of economic domination and social exclusion, which violently insert our bodies into the alienating morass of an intensified global division of labor. In concert with Marx, Freire understood that hegemonic schooling is founded on a pedagogy of estrangement, which like that of estranged labor functions to alienate students from their bodies and the natural world.

Freire (1998a) considered this estrangement of the body akin to "that invisible power of alienating domestication . . . a state of refined estrangement, of the mind's abdication of its own essential self, of a loss of consciousness of the body, of a 'mass production' of the individual, and of conformity" (p. 102). The traditional classroom exists as an arena of domestication, where abstract knowledge and its construction are objectified, along with the students who must acquiesce to its alienating function, limiting rationality, and technocratic instrumentalism. Here, the production of knowledge is neither engaged as historical, collective, or embodied phenomenon. Ignored is the obvious fact that our lives unfold within the vital experiences of the flesh and its sentient capacity. "The flesh, the material aspect of the body, is seen as a hindrance which must be overcome, negated, and transcended" (Beckey, 2000, p. 71). This transcending view sidelines the affective and relational needs of student bodies that must endure, resist, and struggle to become free from the social and material entanglements of a society that imprisons them, both ideologically and corporally.

The historical absence of the body in the classroom is likely due to institutional fears associated with the body's real potential for disruption and subversion. For this reason, a political commitment to counter the disembodiment of our humanity is at the heart of Freire's pedagogy of love. To endure daily confrontations with oppressive forces, for example, Freire (1998a) urged us to

> struggle for the material conditions without which our body will suffer from neglect, thus running the risk of becoming frustrated and ineffective, then [we] will no longer be the witness that [we] ought to be, no longer the tenacious fighter who may tire but who never gives us.
>
> (p. 95)

Yet, missing from educational discourses is precisely this political connection of the body to the critical formation, for both teachers and students. Nevertheless, Freire (1993) embraced the totality of the body in the act of knowing, insisting, "It is my entire body that socially knows. I cannot, in the name of exactness and rigor, negate my body, my emotions and my feelings" (p. 105).

Despite Freire's assertion, most teacher preparation programs seldom engage substantively the manner in which students' physical responses can serve as meaningful indications in assessing more accurately their academic needs. No matter the age or grade level, students can experience and express, overtly or covertly, responses of excitement, frustration, joy, and despair in the process of their learning. Freire (1998b) considered these emotions as logical human responses, in that "studying is a demanding occupation, in the process of which we will encounter pain, pleasure, victory, defeat, doubt and happiness" (p. 78). When these responses are ignored, pedagogical practices default into domestication, silencing the creativity and imagination rooted in the wisdom of the body.

Thus, as a political and organic entity, the body plays a significant role in making sense of the material conditions and social relations of power that shape our lives. Similarly, a praxis of the body can support teachers in building a democratic educational practice, where students are not asked to confront themselves and each other as strangers, but rather through the spirit of human kinship and community, from the moment they enter the classroom. True to this view, a pedagogy of love seeks to engage, in the flesh, the embodied histories and knowledges of the oppressed, as well as the repressive circumstances that inhibit their voice, social agency, self-determination, and solidarity. From this liberatory position, Freire (1993) again spoke to the undeniable centrality of the body in the act of knowing the world:

> The importance of the body is indisputable; the body moves, acts, rememorizes, the struggle for its liberation; the body in sum, desires,

points out, announces, protests, curves itself, rises, designs and remakes the world . . . and its importance has to do with a certain sensualism . . . contained by the body, even in connection with cognitive ability . . . its absurd to separate the rigorous acts of knowing the world from the [body's] passionate ability to know.

(p. 87)

Unfortunately, and worth repeating, it is the power of this sensualism, with its revolutionary potential to summon dissent and nurture the empowerment of students, that is systematically stripped away from the educational process of hegemonic schooling. In response, Freire's view of the body challenged conservative ideologies of social control, historically associated with a Puritanical epistemicide that considers the body as evil, sensual pleasure as sinful, and passions as corrupting to the sanctity of the spirit—all underlying notions reflected in the pedagogical policies and practices within schools today. On this, Freire noted how the sensuality of the body is fettered and confined within schools, discouraged from expression and the freedom to be.

Similarly, the hegemonic tradition of fettered bodies is also product of an educational tradition rooted in the convergence of three dominant paradigms of the West, represented by Socrates, Christianity, and behavioral psychology. In the classical Socratic tradition, the sensual body is quickly subordinated to the mind, while ideas are privileged over the senses (Seidel, 1964). In Christianity, the separation between the body and the soul constitutes the whole relation to learning. In the behaviorist model, the body is transformed into an instrumentalized object to be manipulated and dominated through external stimulus, in the process of learning.

These views of teaching and learning have historically led to pedagogical practices that do violence through an erasure of the body and the annihilation of the flesh in the act of knowing. Accordingly, inequalities are reproduced through class, racialized, gendered, ableist, and heterosexist perceptions and distortions, which are embedded, wittingly or unwittingly, in prevailing attitudes of most well-meaning teachers. Implicit here are deficit assumptions and debilitating preconceptions projected upon students seen to be outside the classed, racialized, patriarchal, hetero-normative, abled, or spiritual mainstream. Consequently, students from working class and racialized communities, where the body's spontaneity is given greater primacy and freedom in the act of knowing, are often expected to sacrifice the creative and sensual knowledge of their bodies to an atomized, abstracted, and dispassionate logic of being. Accordingly, the body's sexuality is repressed as an unwelcome intrusion to the regimen of classroom life.

This ill-fated disembodiment begins early in students' academic formation, resulting in a troubling dichotomy between the body and mind in students' reading of the world. Freire (2005) problematized this dichotomy, given the necessity for students to learn how to *read our bodies,* in the course of their political formation.

> Issues of sociability, imagination, feelings, desires, fear, courage, love, hate, raw anger, sexuality, and so on lead us to the need to "read" our bodies as if they were texts, through the interrelations that make-up their whole. There is the need for an interdisciplinary reading of bodies with students, for breaking away from dichotomies, ruptures that are enviable and deforming.
>
> (p. 52)

It is worth noting here that Freire's own passionate way of being in the world and the variety of references he made to the "beauty of the body" and "the restlessness of bodies" also bears witness to an appreciation for the sensuality and sexuality of human beings. He insisted that "sexuality has a determining effect on the development of consciousness and reason" (Spring 1994). In *Pedagogy of the Heart,* Freire (1997) commented on the "gradual improvement in performance on the part of the students, as the pedagogy of questioning started to gain ground against the pedagogy of answers, and as issues around the body were addressed in the Sexual Orientation Program" (p. 62)—a program that was in place during his post as Secretary of Education for the city of São Paulo.

Given the significant role of the body in the pedagogical process, the Western epistemological severing of the body in the construction of knowledge interferes dramatically with students' capacities to know themselves, one another, and their world. Repressive views of the body and sexuality within education also serve to negate, overtly or covertly, the cultural knowledges of oppressed cultural populations, whose epistemological views and expressions of the body in the cultural process of their knowing may differ substantially from the mainstream's dichotomization of body and consciousness. In the process, this can also render teachers and students alienated and estranged from forms of human suffering that exist outside of the limited scope of the hegemonic lens, whether this is linked to class, gender, ethnicity, sexuality, skin color, physical constitution, or spiritual beliefs.

With this in mind, it is interesting to note that despite human development theories that affirm we are sexual beings even in the womb, serious engagement with human sexuality is systematically repressed and denied in U.S. classrooms. This is so even at puberty, when students' bodies are experiencing heightened and confusing sensations. Seldom do teachers—many who are not particularly comfortable with their own sexuality—critically engage the question of sexuality, beyond repeated clichés of "raging hormones" in reference to teenage sexuality. In the process, students are not only pedagogically abandoned, but also left at the mercy of the media and corporate pirates that, very deliberately and systematically, prey upon the powerful sensations, emotions, and stirrings of youth. In the culture industry of advertising, for example, teenage bodies are sought after for the exchange value they generate in marketing an adolescent sexuality, which offers a marginal exoticism and ample pleasures to the largely male consumer. Commodification reifies and fixates the complexity of youth bodies and the range of possibilities they might assume, while simultaneously exploiting them as fodder for the marketplace (Giroux, 1998).

Frightened by their own ambivalence and the physicality of student bodies, educational policy makers and educators institute practices that systematically silence physical expression, rigidly limiting any discussion of one of the most significant aspects of our humanity. The message is clear; teachers and students are expected to leave their sexuality, along with all other aspects of their cultural knowledge and lived histories at the door, prior to entering. Yet, despite the difficulties and hardships that such silence portends for many students—isolation and increasing rates of suicide among many LBGTQ youth, for example—schools and teachers, much like the fundamentalist church, function as moralistic agents to police and repress the body's participation, in ways that leave students uninformed about the important role of the body in the struggle for consciousness and liberation.

Yet in spite of major institutional efforts to repress and control the desires, pleasures and mobility of the body within classrooms and society, Freire writings support the view that students seldom surrender their bodies completely or readily acquiesce to authoritarian practices—practices which in themselves provide the impetus for resistance, especially in those students whose dynamic histories are excluded within mainstream education. Instead, Freire (1970b) recognized that in their struggle for freedom, those who are repressed, including youth, will "try out forms of rebellious action" (p. 64). As such, many engage in the construction of their own cultural forms of resistance that may or may not always function in their best interest.

Often, expressions of student resistance are enacted through alterations of the body—be they clothing, hairstyle, posturing, manner of walking, way of speaking, the piercing and tattooing of the body. These actions represent then not only acts of resistance but also alternative ways of experiencing, affirming, and knowing the world, generally perceived by officials as transgressive and disruptive to the social order. In a footnote in *Pedagogy of the Oppressed*, Freire (2005) made reference to this phenomenon.

> Young people increasingly view parent and teacher authoritarianism as inimical to their own freedom. For this very reason, they increasingly oppose forms of action which minimize their expressiveness and hinder their self-affirmation. This very positive phenomenon is not accidental. It is actually a symptom of the historical climate . . . For this reason one cannot (unless he [or she] has a personal interest in doing so) see the youth rebellion as a mere example of the traditional differences between generations. Something deeper is involved here. Young people in their rebellion are denouncing and

condemning the unjust model of a society of domination. This rebellion with its special dimension, however, is very recent; society continues to be authoritarian in character.

(p. 154)

Such authoritarian views of students are also exacerbated by
a "new form of representational politics [that] has emerged in
media culture fueled by degrading visual depictions of youth
as criminal, sexually decadent, drug crazed, and illiterate.
In short, youth are viewed as a growing threat to the public
order" (Giroux, 1998).[2]

Teachers, whose bodies are similarly restricted, alienated
and domesticated by their workplace, are under enormous
pressure to follow strict policies and procedures for classroom
conduct, instead of employing more creative and humanizing
approaches, grounded in the actual needs of their students.
Given the impact of disembodied practices, teachers generally
experience an uphill battle in meeting standardized mandates,
which systematically extricate student bodies from the equa-
tion of their learning. Moreover, educators who struggle in
this repressive context to implement liberating strategies are
often forced to become masters of deception—saying what the
principal or district office wishes to hear, while doing behind
closed doors what they believe is in the best interest of students.
Unfortunately, having to shoulder the physical stress of this
duplicity can drive some of the most effective teachers away
from their chosen vocation, given the intolerable alienation
this engenders. Others, who simply feel defeated or frustrated
by the pressure, adopt more authoritarian approaches to
that manipulate or coerce *cooperation,* justifying their decision with contradictory rhetoric about pragmatic necessity.
What cannot be overlooked is that authoritarian practices of

the classroom not only "blindfold students and lead them to a domesticated future" (Freire, 1970b, p. 79), but also alienate teacher labor as well.

Freire's view of the body is also salient to rethinking university education, where there seems to be little pedagogical tolerance for the emotional needs of adult learners. "Somewhere in the intellectual history of the West there developed the wrongheaded idea that mind and heart are antagonists, that scholarship must be divested of emotion, that spiritual journeys must avoid intellectual concerns" (Lifton, 1990, p. 29). This tradition sets an expectation that professors and students compartmentalize themselves within the classroom, without serious attention to the manner in which the very essence of university education is often tied to crucial moments of life transition; and even more so for working class students of color who may be the first generation to attend university.

Simultaneously, students are expected to enter their studies or research as objective, distanced, and impartial observers, even when the object of their study may be linked intimately to brutal conditions of human suffering, are a part of their lived histories. Freire (1993) rightly argued that traditional academic expectations of the university affirm "that feelings corrupt research and its findings, the fear of intuition, the categorical negation of emotion and passion, the belief in technicism, [which] ends in convincing many that, the more neutral we are in our actions, the more objective and efficient we will be" (p. 106) in our construction of knowledge. Hence, students are slowly but surely socialized to labor as uncritical, descriptive, "neutral" scholars, dispassionate and alienated from their subject of study. The result is often scholarship conceived epistemologically in a deeply *estranged* way, devoid of the very qualities that comprise our humanity. The unfortunate consequence here is that disembodied knowledge seldom leads teachers and students to grapple critically with deeper moral questions of education, which would undoubtedly challenge social and material relations that sustain human suffering and structural inequalities, in the first place.

Freire (1983) affirmed that we possess *a conscious body*, indispensable to the evolution of critical consciousness. "His or her consciousness, with its 'intentionality' towards the world, is always conscious of something. It is in a permanent state of moving towards reality. Hence, the condition of the human being is to be in constant relationship to the world" (p. 146). The dialectical relationships between the body and consciousness, object and subject, students and the world are essential to both a critical understanding of the world and forging actions that can have material consequences on the lives of the oppressed. Similarly, Freire believed that transformation of the social and material structures of oppression could not be undertaken by mere abstraction devoid of action; nor could emancipatory action result devoid of the love that moves us toward social consciousness. For Freire, the greatest emancipatory potential that underlies a pedagogy of love is the integral enactment of our human faculties—body, mind, heart, and spirit—in our pedagogical and political struggles to awaken critical consciousness.

Notes

1 See interview with Etiene Balibar conducted by Clement Petitjean on April 15, 2014, available at www.versobooks.com/blogs/1559-a-racism-without-races
2 See Giroux, H. (1998). Teenage Sexuality, Body Politics and the Pedagogy of Display. Available at www.henryagiroux.com/online_articles/teenage_sexuality.htm

3

CONSCIENTIZAÇAO: AWAKENING CRITICAL CONSCIOUSNESS

Conscientizaçao represents the development of the awakening of critical awareness.

—Paulo Freire (1983)

Freire's pedagogy of love invites educators to embrace the struggle for critical consciousness and social transformation as a road yet to be made, which, because it is unknown, must be traced out step-by-step, in our organic relationship with the world and in the process of our labor as educators, activists, and revolutionary leaders. The struggle for change begins, then, at the moment when human beings become both critically aware and intolerant of the oppressive conditions in which they find themselves and push toward new ways of knowing and being in the world. This process signals that moment of consciousness when individuals in community experience a breakthrough and decide to take another path, despite their uncertain future. Freire (1998a) considered the process of conscientization an essential critical principle of his pedagogy, in that it opens the field for the expression of epistemological curiosity hence, "it is one of the roads we have to follow if we are to deepen our awareness of the world, of facts, of events" (p. 55). Similarly, Freire's notion of human consciousness, as unfinished, offers us a sense of *conscientizaçao* as a critical evolutionary process, whose openness can enliven our dialectical relationship with the world and beckons us toward emancipatory futures.

The evolution of conscientizaçao or social consciousness is well echoed by the metaphor *el camino se hace al andar*[1] or *we make the road by walking*. Freire, in dialogue with Myles Horton (Horton & Freire, 1990), spoke adamantly of social consciousness as a dialectical process that develops and evolves, as we each contend, through theory and practice, with the actual social conditions we find before us and in relationship with others. Rather than adhere to prescribed roles and structures that oppress and repress our humanity, Freire (1998a) urged for the development of emancipatory consciousness, through a critical praxis that requires our ongoing participation as cultural citizens and subjects of the world. From this perspective, knowledge and the breakthroughs of consciousness it informs emanate critically and reflect the evolving social experience of the people themselves. And so, he asserted that our moments of awakening to critical consciousness or "the breakthrough of a new form of awareness in understanding the world is not the privilege of one person. The experience that makes possible the 'breakthrough' is a collective experience" (p. 77).

True to his own understanding of knowledge as historical, there was a deepening in Freire's articulation of the awakening consciousness or conscientizaçao, over the years. This is particularly the case in his later writings, where he gave far greater salience to the role of feelings, sensations, and the body, in addition to the exercise of reason, in the formation of consciousness. This is particularly evident in *Pedagogy of Freedom*, when Freire (1998b) asserts that "[w]hat is important in teaching is not the mechanical repetition of this or that gesture but a comprehension of the value of sentiments, emotions, and desires . . . and sensibility, affectivity, and intuition" (p. 48). This powerful assertion of the value of our human faculties, beyond our reason, in the struggle for our liberation is a hallmark of Freire's pedagogy of love. His painstaking efforts to challenge the necrophilic grip of hegemonic schooling, simultaneously, pushed forth a new integral rationality infused with a communal understanding of social consciousness or *conscientizaçao* as a living phenomenon of women and men in struggle.

Concept of Conscientizaçao

> It is sufficient to know that conscientization does not take place in abstract beings in the air but in real men and women and in social structures, to understand that it cannot remain on the level of the individual.
>
> —Paulo Freire (1983)

Freire's concept of conscientizaçao points to an understanding of critical awareness and the formation of social consciousness as both a historical phenomenon and a human social process connected to our communal capacities to become authors and social actors of our destinies. In *Education for Critical Consciousness*, Freire (1983) distinguished what he considered to be the three forms of consciousness: semi-intransitive, transitive, and critical transitive. In the process of conscientização, he believed that consciousness undergoes a movement or evolution that proceeds, first, from *semi-transitive consciousness* or a place where the predominant focus of individuals is placed on their survival and limited engagement as subjects of a larger historical process. Here the oppressed may tend to be inadvertently identified with the dominant ideology, in that our very survival is tied to the wiles and interests of the powerful.

Freire asserted that as individuals begin to extend our awareness out into the world, we tend to respond in ways that reflect a *transitive consciousness,* which is most characterized by a permeability that increases our capacity to enter into dialogue with others and extend ourselves beyond merely a preoccupation with our immediate survival. Lastly, Freire theorized that individuals move toward expressions of *critical transitive consciousness,* which he characterized by greater dialectical depth in our interpretation of problems and the world, increasing our capacity for critical engagement, the problematizing of commonsensical notions and conditions, an openness to revisioning, a rejection of passivity, and an empowered ability to enter into the practice of critical reflection and dialogue. This process, he surmised, is propelled through participation in critical dialogue and ongoing emancipatory actions, in the name of social transformation.

Freire, however, makes a point to emphasize that conscientização does not occur automatically, naturally, nor should it be understood as an evolving linear phenomenon. Instead, he spoke to an emancipatory consciousness that arises through an organic process of human engagement, which requires critical pedagogical interactions that nurture the dialectical relationship of human beings with the world. This entails a grounded appreciation for the dialectical tension that must be retained, between the empowerment of the individual and the democratic well-being of the larger communal sphere. In an interview with Rex Davis (1981), Freire spoke to the significance of this *dialecticity*.

> Only when we understand the "dialecticity" between consciousness and the world—that is, when we know that we don't have a consciousness here and the world there but, on the contrary, when both of them, the objectivity and the subjectivity, are incarnating dialectically, is it possible to understand what *conscientização* is, and to understand the role of consciousness in the liberation of humanity.
>
> (p. 62)

In writing about critical consciousness, Freire also anchors his conceptual meaning of conscientização based upon several key notions. First, he explains that the more accurately human beings can grasp the true causality of our particular circumstances or conditions of life, the more critical our understanding of reality will be. Yet, he provided an important caveat here. That is, whatever is considered true today may not necessarily be true tomorrow. Freire posits here a historical and dialectical theory of meaning that must be understood both relationally and contextually. As history moves and conditions shift, so must our readings of world, if we are to enable emancipatory life. The second notion is an outcome of the first, in that critical awareness encompasses phenomena or facts that exist empirically or experientially within particular circumstances that inform their production. As such, through a critical awareness of the world, as rooted in particular social and economic conditions of life, we can more readily come to comprehend consciousness and the actions it informs as corresponding phenomena. Inherent to this view of the world is an inseparability between consciousness and materiality that must be acknowledged and dialectically sustained. And lastly, but similar to the latter, the nature of human actions and societal structures corresponds to the nature of prevailing epistemologies and ideologies that inform structures for communal life.

Freire's notion of conscientizaçao entails the organic formation of an intimate relationship between consciousness, human action, and the world that we seek to reinvent. But most important, he emphasizes the communal or social circumstances that are required in its formation. Freire (1983) explained the deepening of this *prise de conscience*[2] in the following manner:

> [It] is not and never can be an intellectual or an intellectualist effort. Conscientization cannot be arrived at by a psychological, idealist subjectivist road, nor through objectivism . . . Just as the *prise de conscience* cannot operate in isolated individuals, but through the relations of transformation they establish between themselves and the world . . . [it] results . . . in a person's coming face to face with the world and with concrete reality . . . This effort of the *prise de conscience* to transcend itself and achieve conscientization, which always requires one's critical insertion in the reality which one begins to unveil, cannot be individual but social.
>
> (p. 148)

A powerful political dimension to the process of conscientizaçao worth repeating is that critical consciousness, although it takes place in and emerges out of the expressed lived histories of each individual, cannot evolve and transform in the absence of others. More specifically, Freire argued that "we cannot liberate the others, people cannot liberate themselves alone, because people liberate themselves in communion, mediated by reality which they must transform" (Davis, 1981, p. 62). Also of note here is that Freire understood exceedingly well that the concept of conscientizaçao could be easily distorted. In the first, through a sort of humanist idealism and liberal subjectivism that strips the concept of its criticality. Privileging subjectively, it produces truths divorced from social and material conditions. In the second, scientific objectivity reigns supreme, privileging objectively produced truths, divorced from social and material conditions. In both instances, forms of consciousness result from a dichotomy of the subject/object relationship, in the process of knowing, rather than critically from a socially grounded interdependence of subject and object.

In contrast, the process of conscientizaçao or conscientization evolves from the ongoing dialectical relationship between human beings and the world. In this view, we come to consciousness through a widening capacity to exercise an integral rationality. One in which subjective and objective knowledge, mind and body, matter and spirit, human beings and the natural world coexist in a perpetual dance, which resists their negation. Counterpunctal to this negation, Freire (1998a) argued, "human existence is, in fact, a radical and profound tension between good and evil, between dignity and indignity, between decency and indecency, between beauty and ugliness of the world" (p. 53).

Most important, it is in the midst of this dialectical tension in the process of learning that epistemological curiosity unfolds. Freire (1998a) often connected his critical understanding of conscientization to the notion of epistemological curiosity. He defined this curiosity as,

> restless questioning, as movement toward the revelation of something hidden, as a question verbalized or not, as search for clarity, as a moment of attention, suggestion, and vigilance, [which] constitutes an integral part of the phenomenon of being alive. There could be no creativity without curiosity that moves us and sets us patiently impatient before a world that we did not make, to add to it something of our own making.
>
> (pp. 37–38)

Learning as a critical dialogical process for the formation of consciousness then must open the field to an active and rigorous investigation beyond simply our intuition or hunch—although Freire (1998a) valued the significant contribution of these to learning. But, rather than stopping there, he urged us to "build on our intuitions and submit them to methodological and rigorous analysis so that our curiosity becomes epistemological" (p. 48), and in so doing, we uncover those actions that are in the service of transformation.

Through critical dialogue, where our "curiosity becomes epistemological," there is room for its expression, as well as the necessity to consider rigorously its meaning, in relationship to the world. In this way, Freire (1998a) maintained the dialectical tension between two important epistemological moments that support the development of consciousness: the necessity "to be immersed in existing knowledge as it is and to be open and capable of producing something that does not yet exist" (p. 35). Given the oppressive policies and practices that defile emancipatory efforts within schools and society, Freire adamantly argued that we could not leave behind our critical consciousness when contending with the bombardment of commonsensical notions meant to conserve recalcitrant structures of oppression. As such, the phenomenon of conscientizaçao is also deeply informed by our capacity to enter into the problematization of hegemony.

Problematization

> Liberation implies the problematization of their situation in its concrete objective reality so that being critically aware of it, they can also act critically on it.
>
> —Paulo Freire (1983)

One can only know to the extent that one has the opportunity and freedom to problematize the conditions and realities in which we are immersed. "To present this human world as a problem for human beings is to propose that they 'enter into' it critically, taking the operation as a whole, their action and that of others on it" (p. 155). By entering into their own world, students can become aware of what they know in relation to their world and also what more they need to know, in order to participate more concretely, in the making of their destinies. This is a path toward greater consciousness, where students are actively involved in the task of codifying their reality as they know it and moving beyond the known to the unknown, toward becoming creators of knowledge and participants in making of the world. Freire believed that through an ongoing dialogical process of problem posing or problematization, with students as subjects of their own learning, critical consciousness evolves and, as such, students organically participate in altering their lives, both as individuals and collective beings. In Freire's pedagogy of love, students learn to exercise their reason in ways that lead to the construction of integral knowledge, which opens the door to further questioning and greater curiosity of why the world is as it is and how it might be different.

An important aspect of the pedagogy here is for students to find genuine opportunities for voice and democratic participation, in which they can think through more deeply the consequences of their individual and collective attitudes, interventions, behaviors, decisions, and most important, the relationship of these to the official standards of knowledge imposed by hegemonic schooling. This implies a process of learning not necessarily dependent on a specific or determined curriculum per se, but far more concerned with the capacity of educators creating the pedagogical conditions for problematization, so students can critically question, deconstruct, and recreate knowledge without repercussions or reprisals, in ways that enhance their sense of ethical responsibility to self and community.

Inherent to this problem-posing approach is a pedagogical process that humanizes; in that, according to Freire (1983), "to be human is to engage in relationships with others and with the world" (p. 3). However, beyond the subjective humanizing dimension, he also insisted that a humanizing pedagogy guides students "to experience that world as an objective reality, independent of oneself, capable of being known" (p. 3). Thus, through ongoing participation in problem-posing dialogue, students gradually undergo an integral process of social and political formation. In so doing, they come to understand in profound ways that human beings concretely make the world and thus, as human beings, they must also act concretely to transform it. Highlighting this point, Freire (1993) contended that

> problematization is not an intellectual diversion, both alienated and alienating. Nor is it an escape from action, a way of disguising the

fact that what is real has been denied. Problematization is not only inseparable from the act of knowing but also inseparable from concrete situations.

(p. 153)

This inseparability from concrete situations or material conditions is key to understanding why social consciousness deepens as students interact with one another and their environment in the dynamic of critical dialogue. More specifically, by critically engaging with official or commonsensical knowledge, creating and recreating that content by their integral participation, responding to the challenges it poses, stepping outside egoism to consider the impact on others, students come to question: In favor of what? In favor of whom? (A. M. A. Freire, 1995). Discerning the social and material consequences to transcend limit situations, students come to know the essence of themselves as full subjects of history, rather than objects to be manipulated, prescribed, exploited, or dominated.

Noteworthy here are two important features related to problematization that must remain at the forefront. First is the dialectical nature of the teacher-student relationship, which must be upheld in the dialogical process of problematization; in that, Freire argued that teachers and students must enter together through dialogue into the process of social change, whereby conscientizing both themselves and students simultaneously in a process of *interconscientization*. On this, Freire (1983) wrote,

Problematization is so much a dialectical process that it would be impossible for anyone to begin it without becoming involved in it. No one can present something to someone else as a problem and at

the same time remain a mere spectator of the process . . . In the process of problematization, any step made by a Subject to penetrate
the problem-situation continually opens up new roads for others
subjects to comprehend the object being analyzed . . . The humbler
they are in this process the more they will learn.

(p. 153)

This collective or social feature must be absolutely central to
how we, as educators, activists, and community leaders comprehend Freire's principle of conscientizaçao.

Second is the historical question; in that Freire (1998a)
firmly believed that "to the degree that the historical past is
not 'problematized' so as to be critically understood, tomorrow becomes simply *the* perpetuation of today" (p. 102). To
counter this outcome, requires a process of problematization
that is integrated within a critical praxis of dialogue. As such,
he believed deeply that through democratic forms of horizontal engagement, where I-Thou relationships of historical subjects reside, love, humility, trust, and criticality can prevail. In
this process of knowing, students learn how to enact reflection
and action in a permanent alliance, through the communal
process of dialogue.

Dialogue and Conscientization

If it is in speaking their word that people, by naming the world, transform it, dialogue imposes itself as the way by which they achieve significance as human beings. Dialogue is thus an existential necessity.

—Paulo Freire (1970b)

In concert with the gnosiological and historical dimensions of
reason, Freire (1983) considered dialogue to be indispensable

to the act of knowing the world and hence, to the process of conscientization. It is through critical dialogue that students enter together into the process of problematization. And, by way of their critical exchanges, they experience important breakthroughs of knowledge that emerge from their rethinking of historical and contemporary conditions. Within this process of reflection, new actions can emerge that better support students to participate more substantively in the process of their own learning, as well as enhance their experience of democracy, within culturally democratic relationships that focus on equality and justice. Another way to think of this phenomenon is that through engaging new possibilities in the process of teaching and learning, students are involved in potentially reconfiguring asymmetrical power relations, in order to enact greater horizontal relationships, structures, and practices within the classroom and beyond.

Freire also placed much importance on students experiencing conditions in the classroom that nurture their intimacy with the practice of democracy. For he believed that it is through a deeply experiential and integral learning of democracy, in body, mind, heart, and spirit, that students come to understand that democracy is never a given and "liberation is not a gift" (Davis 1981, p. 62). Rather, democracy is an active collective human project that must be consistently reconsidered, regenerated, and reinvented, through our vigilance and engagement with the actual historical and material conditions that impact our lives as individuals and cultural beings. Moreover, Freire (1983) believed that the proper climate to practice *an apprenticeship democracy* is within the openness of dialogue, where men and women can develop a sense of community and participation in the solution of common life. This entails a consciousness of social and political responsibility, which grows and matures through meaningful and purposeful civic participation.

Freire asserted that "consciousness is intentionality towards the world" (Davis, 1981, p. 58), and critical dialogue is the means by which that intentionality is forged. Hence, we must seek to act, think, and speak about our reality in ways that are coherent with emancipatory principles of life, which insert teachers and students into a process of ongoing mediation. As a politically dynamic process, critical dialogue also serves as an essential means by which we can bring greater congruence to our thoughts and actions as coparticipants in the world. About this, Freire (1983) posited that since thinking human beings do not think alone, "[t]here is no longer an 'I think' but 'we think.' It is the 'we think' which establishes the 'I think' and not the contrary" (p. 137). This necessary coparticipation of the Subject in the act of critical thought constitutes a significant break with the dualism of Descartes and invites us to embrace an emancipatory understanding of knowledge construction as both communal and contextual, given that it must be anchored within the shared conditions that inform the lives of knowing Subjects.

And, as such, we must understand dialogue as both a meaningful form of communication and active process of learning that retains a reciprocity which cannot be broken. In this reciprocal relationship of coconstructing knowledge and the world, students encounter genuine opportunities to direct their entrance into the classroom dialogue in meaningful ways. This in turn calls upon educators to assume pedagogical responsibility for employing culturally appropriate and creative ways to engage students with respect to "mandatory knowledge" and classroom expectations, in order to ensure that a dialogical reciprocity persists in the teaching and learning process.

A common break in this reciprocity is precisely what occurs in the banking model of education or training, where the teacher is expected to teach and students to learn, without any recognition that true learning is a communal process, which must be reciprocal if it is to support the critical formation of oppressed students and their communities. Hence, it becomes more evident why deficit notions of education work antidialogically and, thus, thwart the process of conscientization, rendering students passive agents in traditional learning environments. Freire (1970b) sought to unveiled how deficit notions undergird *false generosity,* by "softening" the domination of the powerful, by essentializing the weaknesses of the oppressed to justify a culture of exclusion and domination. Of this he said,

> The dominating consciousness absolutizes ignorance in order to manipulate the so-called "uncultured." If some men [and women] are "totally ignorant," they will be incapable of managing themselves, and will need the orientation, the "direction," the "leadership" of those who consider themselves to be "cultured" and "superior."
>
> (p. 43)

Freire considered this *absolutizing of ignorance* as simply part of a larger antidialogical process, where myths are normalized and employed by the dominant culture to suppress the social agency and civic participation of subordinated populations. Here, he spoke to the manner in which the world is *mythicized* by the powerful, in order to ensure the alienation, passivity, and domestication of the oppressed. In the process, a series of myths and corresponding policies, practices, and methods are enacted to preclude the problematization of the world. Instead, social and material conditions of inequality, for example, are treated as fixed and naturalized phenomena to which subordinate cultural populations must simply adapt. Freire (1970b) provided pointed examples of myths indispensable to the preservation of the status quo.

> [F]or example, the myth that the oppressive order is a "free society"; the myth that all persons are free to work where they wish, that if they don't like their boss they can leave him and look for another job; the myth that this order respects human rights and is therefore worthy of esteem; the myth that anyone who is industrious can become an entrepreneur—worse yet, the myth that the street vendor is as much an entrepreneur as the owner of a large factory; the myth of the universal right of education, when . . . only a tiny fraction ever reach the university; the myth of the equality of all individuals, when the question: "Do you know who you're talking to?" is still current among us; the myth of the heroism of the oppressor classes as defenders of "Western Christian civilization" against "materialist barbarism"; the myth of the charity and generosity of the elites, when what they really do as a class is to foster selective "good deeds" . . . the myth that the dominant elites, 'recognizing their duties,' promote the advancement of the people, so that the people, in a gesture of gratitude, should accept the words of the elites and be conformed to them; the myth that rebellion is a sin against God; the myth of private property as fundamental to personal human development (so long as oppressors are the only true human beings); the myth of the industriousness of the oppressors and the laziness and dishonesty of the oppressed, as well as the myth of the natural inferiority of the latter and the superiority of the former
>
> (pp. 39–41)

Hence, Freire asserted that a decolonizing pedagogy requires the *demythologizing of reality,* to counter the domestication of consciousness, inherent in banking education. For example, one of the most debilitating hegemonic myths has been the view of education as a neutral enterprise. In response, Freire persistently challenged disingenuous notions of neutrality within schools and society that veil underlying structures of inequality. He adamantly argued that if we are in constant interaction with the world, is impossible to maintain a posture of neutrality. Therefore, he surmised, "if we are conscious or not as educators, our praxis is either for the liberation of the people—their humanization—or for their domestication, their domination" (Davis, 1981, p. 57).

Although Freire's own formation was grounded in the intellectual roots of Western philosophy, his theorizing went beyond the neutrality of Socratic principles of dialogue or Plato's realm of transcendence. As educators, activists, scholars, and leaders committed to the struggle for our humanity, Freire firmly believed that our connection and contact with the world is essential to a politics of change. He argued dialectically against neutrality, while also calling forth the "openness of the future" that must extend beyond certitudes, sectarianism, or dogma. For those socialized deeply within Western positivism, this negation of neutrality on one end and the assertion of openness on the other can boggle the mind. Yet, Freire's dialectical stance speaks to both personal and political levels of struggle. On the personal level, grounded in an emancipatory political vision, we must struggle fiercely against forms of sectarianism or dogma that render us rigid and close-minded to the creative and unforeseen possibilities for social change. Yet, on the political arena, we cannot pretend that most mainstream policies and practices are not ideologically encumbered by repressive epistemologies or epistemicides that, wittingly or unwittingly, adhere to the interests of the wealthy and powerful.

Hence, it is not surprising that under the guise of political neutrality, benevolent control, and educational expediency, many public policies and practices of schooling (i.e., testing, tracking, standardizations of knowledge, etc.) perpetuate class privilege and racialized ideological structures, among other forms of social exclusions, which historically have turned a blind eye to the exploitation and domination of the majority of the world's population. Hence, to call for neutrality or even "balance " in political and pedagogical contexts, where the struggle for decolonization is central to our humanity, constitutes a cowardly act that disingenuously abandons our responsibility as cultural citizens committed to social justice and culturally democratic life.

Moreover, Freire (1995) linked the question of neutrality to his discussion of *directivity*, in that the concept exposes "the impossibility of being neutral in the practice of education" (p. 18). For Freire, a critical process of education implies the transformation and evolution in our understanding of the world. Hence, it also implies a movement toward critical utopian dreams, desires, and values. However, this is neither a liberal view of schooling that upholds a relativist conceptualization of education or a quest for a utopian "la la land," where human life is transformed into some paradise of unencumbered freedom. Instead, Freire cautioned us that democracy is never guaranteed and constitutes an ever-present terrain of struggle. As such, human pathologies related to power are always a real possibility and require our political vigilance. Our labor in schools and communities then must uphold clarity and openness of political vision and a grounded understanding that human beings must permanently grapple with those powerful dialectical tensions inherent in the constant making and remaking of democracy.

In direct opposition, the politics of hegemonic schooling conserve and reproduce colonizing attitudes and practices founded on reified knowledge and deficit notions, where students are deceptively initiated into static and limited prescribed roles for which the limits of their educational opportunities prepare them to assume. Not surprisingly then that Freire objected to the notion of "training," which renders students and workers passive receptacles of a fragmented, specialized, and instrumentalized knowledge, in which they are not permitted the room for conscientization—a requisite for their full democratic participation. This uncritical process of labor is often essentialized and well supported, on practical grounds, even among those working within oppressed communities, in the name of making a living. Freire (1970b), however, objected; in that, "through such methods the masses are directed and manipulated" (p. 143) and their quest for liberation thwarted. In contrast, if the preparation for particular jobs were accompanied by humanizing opportunities for critical formation, participation in decision making, community involvement, and an emphasis on a livable wage, perhaps a better case could be made for such an approach, as an initial measure. Unfortunately, mainstream "training" programs are generally associated with limited choices, limited voice, and limited wages.

At this juncture, it should be noted that Freire's conceptualization of dialogue as essential to an emancipatory pedagogy and community struggle have not always been accurately understood or practiced by those who would reduce his pedagogy to method, stripping away its revolutionary intent. This is particularly true, given that instrumentalized or functionalist approaches to dialogue destabilize the very principles that give meaning and power to emancipatory life.

For Freire, seeking absolute answers, prescribed formulations, or fixed outcomes are not the intent, when subjects of history enter into communion for the purpose of liberation. This is so, given that under the constraints of capitalism and its sorted inequalities, we are forced to first unveil and problematize the myths and distortions that bind our sensibilities and, from there, move toward collective possibilities often unforeseen at the beginning of our dialogue together. With this in mind, two other important qualities of dialogue include the willingness to exist with uncertainty and to welcome surprise in our encounters. Freire (1970b) considered a critical capacity for uncertainty and surprise important in countering the hegemonic reproduction of *prescription,* where "every prescription represents the imposition of one individual's choice upon another, transforming the consciousness of the person prescribed to into one that conforms" (p. 47).

Given that we have all been so conditioned to hold prescribed expectations of our students or to expect so little from them, classroom opportunities to express their creativity and imagination in more fluid and undetermined ways can result in truly unexpected outcomes. In many ways, what Freire understood is what so many educators accidentally discover— when students genuinely experience the freedom to think and their imaginations find an open field to express themselves, they often work far harder and with greater discipline, enthusiasm, and joy than they do when they are forced into antidialogical modes of teaching that sentence them to prescriptive regurgitation of fixed knowledge—knowledge that is abstracted and decontextualized from their lived histories and their active presence. Traditional tendencies of control and authoritarianism also narrow the field of rationality, by way of prescribed ways of knowing and hegemonic expectations of performance. This privileging of prescribed banking approaches, in turn, diminishes the voices of difference and promotes exclusion. It is the transformation of precisely this deadening and antidialogical pedagogy in schools that informs a problem-posing pedagogy, which advances the formation of consciousness and a democratic culture of voice, participation, and solidarity.

It is worth noting that dialogue that supports the development of emancipatory consciousness does not aspire to creating perfect order in the classroom or the society at large, given that any epistemological and material sense of order is highly ensconced in cultural and class sensibilities, and thus, must remain in the communal terrain of constant renegotiation. Instead, Freire's notion of dialogue aspired to an integral awareness of self and others and an emergence of consciousness, which arms teachers and students with the critical objectivity necessary to allow ourselves and others "to be," so that together we can explore the consequences of relationships and their material circumstances. This process assists us to better read inequalities of power and to discover new possibilities for unfettered expressions of humanity.

Freire also sought through his pedagogy to disrupt the dehumanizing fatalism inherent in a consciousness of oppression, in that his work speaks to the dangers of remaining locked within internalized hegemonic preconceptions of deficiency with respect to the "other." By conforming to a fixed and imposed identity of deficit, Freire saw that this hegemonic internalization become a determining force, disabling our individual and communal capacities to liberate ourselves from the ideological and material conditions of bondage that have been projected or imposed upon us, through forces of repression associated with racism, class inequalities, sexism, disablism, and heterosexism.

Freire proposed dialogue as a terrain of complexities, uncertainties, and ambiguities, where we must risk losing the old definitions of ourselves and the world, in order that we might reinvent it, in ways that affirm the social agency and empower the most disenfranchised. Hence, he anticipated that through dialogue students would begin with a critical interrogation of unexamined assumptions and commonsense notions, for example, about why people are poor, homeless, or unemployed, as well as challenge prepackaged and recycled solutions to poverty based on ignorance. Such interrogations are important, given assumptions about poverty based on oppressive myths—myths that ascribe superiority, entitlement, or privilege to those granted full subjecthood under norms that conserve racialized, patriarchal, and capitalist desires. A decolonizing approach, on the other hand, requires that we confront misguided loyalties to economic values that normalize or mythicize abject poverty, unprecedented incarceration, perpetual war, and a host of other economically bound conditions of human suffering.

Indispensability of Resistance

> What is essential is that learners . . . maintain alive the flame of resistance that sharpens their curiosity and stimulates their capacity to risk.
>
> —Paulo Freire (1998a)

In his introduction to *Pedagogy of Freedom,* Stanley Aronowitz (1998) writes that "Freire holds that a humanized society requires cultural freedom, the ability of the individual to choose values and rules of conduct that violate conventional social norms, and, in political and civil society, requires the full participation of *all* of its inhabitants in every aspect of public life" (p. 19). Freire's dialogical approach then sought to challenge debilitating dualisms and untenable binaries that negate, polarize, or limit life choices. However, to *violate conventional social norms* entails that, by necessity, resistance or dissent must have a place in a democratic society. Hence, student resistance in the classroom merits critical engagement, in that it plays an important role in the process of problematization. Rather than adversarial or problematic to the critical construction of knowledge, resistance serves as meaningful antecedent to the evolution of critical consciousness.

Freire (1983) believed that no problem or act of resistance can ever be resolved by simply ignoring, dismissing, or trying to eliminate the resistance or opposition, without falling into authoritarianism. Instead, what we as teachers must learn to do is to cultivate and nurture dialogue in ways that create new fields of possibility large enough to welcome the tensions generated by resistance. This enhances the field from which students can launch their energies into emancipatory directions of inquiry, through critique and thoughtful engagement. It is this pedagogical response to resistance that most supports the communal evolution of consciousness, in that transformation is made possible through a collective democratic process of participation, voice, solidarity, and action that forges new possibilities.

Accordingly, an important aim of Freire's emancipatory pedagogy is to override preconditioned or hegemonic patterns in how we name the world, by providing a demythologizing context in which teachers and students can consider the political implications of particular ways of thinking and their consequences. In the process, Freire asked us to move away from fixed or prescribed notions of life and toward a relational and contextual understanding of knowledge, history, and community. This idea is also relevant to Freire's (1993) notion of a critical literacy, informed by his teaching of literacy as a decolonizing practice, which for him was "above all, a social and political commitment" (p. 114). In the process of *reading the word and the world,* Freire (2002) also sought to explore "the relationship prevailing between political lucidity . . . and the various levels of engagement in the process of mobilization and organization for struggle—for the defense of rights, for laying claim to justice" (p. 40). Hence, the capacity to read the word and the world is fundamentally linked to a larger political struggle against hegemony, which entails a critical literacy that prepares students toward a more just life.

A problem-posing pedagogy, with Freire's concept of critical literacy as its compass, is meant to support students in becoming consciously aware of their context and their conditions of life; whereby they become more consciously aware of their options and their right to choose, as empowered subjects of their destinies. It is at that point that Freire considered students to become politicized, in that they gained a sense of critical awareness about how power relations impact them and their communities. To become politicized then implies entering into an evolutionary formation of consciousness, by which individuals become critically aware that their active involvement in the historical moment is directly linked to their capacities to denounce injustice and announce a more just world. Resistance here is anchored to a dialogical process by which students or communities struggle to contend with the consequences of particular values, policies, and practices that threaten their right to be. Hence, resistance is often the precursor to students becoming more critically conscious and, as such, must also be linked to an emancipatory right to choice.

Freire's pedagogy encompasses conditions of pedagogy that support teachers, students, and communities to enter intentionally into a lived historical process. Within a pedagogy that supports the development of critical consciousness are also the underlying purposes of empowerment and self-determination that enable students to reflect on their lives and the world around them. Freire (1983) believed that as teachers and students grow in the power of reflection and social agency, we also develop "an increased capacity for choice" (p. 16). This increased capacity for choice is a fundamental prerequisite, as oppressed communities move to liberate ourselves from old prescribed choices that have been handed down to us by the powerful. It is, moreover, through the deepening of consciousness that we recuperate the possibilities for choice.

Freire also made a distinction between *integration* and *adaptation* in the formation of critical consciousness. This conceptual explanation is significant in that it hints to Freire's dislike for the term *marginalization,* in that he did not believe that any of us, whether oppressed or not, could sit at the margins or outside the structures of power. Instead, he insisted that a significant aim of liberation had to be the full participation of the oppressed in the decision making of communities and societies in which we reside. I offer this explanation in that the term *integration* has lost its progressive significance in places like the United States, where the term became more analogous to what Freire called adaption (or in some circles cooptation). More specifically, Freire (1983) explains these terms with respect to the critical capacity to make choices and to act in the interest of transformation.

Integration with one's context, as distinguished from *adaptation,* is a distinctively human activity. Integration results from the capacity to adapt oneself to reality *plus* the critical capacity to make choices and to transform that reality. To the extent that man loses his ability to make choices and is subjected to the choices of others, to the extent that his decisions are no longer his own because they result from external prescriptions, he is no longer integrated. Rather, he is adapted. He has "adjusted."

(p. 4)

Prior to moving forward, it is useful to note that Freire (1983) elsewhere wrote, "to the extent that a person acts more on the basis of emotionality than reason, his behavior occurs adaptively and cannot result in commitment, for committed behavior has its roots in critical consciousness and capacity for genuine choice" (p. 20). However, a similar epistemological concern can be raised to the extent that a person acts far more exclusively or exaggeratedly from the standpoints of pure reason, physicality, or even spirituality, without an integral understanding of the relationship of these human faculties to the formation of meaning and cultural worldviews. Moreover, depending on the cultural and historical milieu from which a basis for knowledge emerges and a particular focus of study evolves, the expression of these human faculties can also echo the cultural needs of students, within a pedagogical context, where the process of conscientization is considered paramount to teaching and learning.

Returning to the question of resistance, Freire (1970a) argued that during epochal transitions, "the deepening of the clash between old and new encouraged a tendency to choose one side or the other; and the emotional climate of the time encouraged the tendency to become radical about the choice"

(p. 10). When intensified this can cause deep polarization in society and also can lead to violence—whether that violence is the oppressor's violence that seeks to preserve the status quo or the violence of the oppressed struggling to create a breakthrough from which new conditions can emerge. This process, of course, can create enormous dissonance and resistance, given that it speaks to the necessity for a significant shift in paradigm. The extent to which educators can express faith, compassion and love for their students, as well as create conditions for all to participate in a process of empowerment, will ultimately determine the manner in which students are able to move through their resistance, when asked to interrogate unjust systems of power and privilege that may implicate their own perspectives and past practices.

This requires educators, prepared to delve into the painful dimensions of personal oppression, to invite students to enter with them into more just ways of being, thinking, and acting—all which may require both teachers and students to undergo continual experiences of both uncertainty and change, as they come to learn from one another that which must be interrogated in the moment. Moreover, it is important that teachers remain open minded and supple in our pedagogical approaches, in that our ideas too can become reified and fixed, losing openness and flexibility in the hardening of our experience, given the frustrations and impatience we can undergo within mainstream educational settings.

It is worth noting here that the dialogical approach of Freire's pedagogy is meant to be as empowering a process for teachers as it is for students, in that it is also meant to prevent teachers from becoming fossilized in our ideas. This is best achieved when we recognize that teaching is as much a process of learning from our students as it is a process of students learning from teachers. Thus, this radical suppleness is best cultivated, as we see in Freire's life, when we aspire persistently to learn with our students, express love and faith in their interactions, and yet, are not afraid to express that "fire in the belly" that is fueled by an uncompromising love for freedom, life, and the world. This process, however, can only proceed effectively, when radical educators have developed sufficient patience, confidence, faith, knowledge, and commitment to a humanizing vision of education. This moves us beyond absolute, reified, and fixed formulas of teaching and learning, toward a dialectical understanding and integral approach, which supports pedagogical practices that bring students and the world into constant relationship, in the interest of democratic life.

Within a Freirian approach to education, resistance then is not considered a problem to be defeated. Instead, a critical understanding of resistance is an essential component to the process by which new knowledge emerges and political formation in the interest of justice evolves. For this reason, Freire (1983) considered the spirit of resistance "a symptom of advancement, an introduction to a more complete humanity [and an] attitude of rebellion as one of the most promising aspects of our political life" (p. 36). However, he did not believe that genuine democratic life could be won by resistance or rebellion alone, in that the struggle for our liberation could not exist predominantly as dissent, but rather had to also move toward a constructive process of critical intervention and remaking of concrete situations. Dialogue, therefore, was for Freire the collective praxis by which we transform the power and promise of resistance into transformative action. So, rather than to shut down resistance by authoritarian means of control or manipulation, Freire urged us to appreciate that without resistance, transformative knowledge is impossible.

This is to say, that resistance holds the key for unveiling, in more substantive ways, the asymmetrical relations of power within schools and society and the impact of oppressive consequences. In essence, resistance can be understood as a significant dialogical juncture, where limit situations can be more clearly identified and unveiled.

By embracing the indispensability of resistance, we come to recognize its relationship to how teachers and students participate either to open the field of rationality or to close it, depending upon ideological allegiances, cultural values, class privilege, or lived histories. An emancipatory response to resistance, through openness and acceptance, expands the field of rationality, in ways that invite students to look more critically at their own attitudes, how these came to be, the consequences of their actions, and new ways in which they might respond to the world, in both theory and practice. This demands a pedagogical process that shifts the focus away from trying to eliminate oppositionalities or resistance to ways that engage student resistance in meaningful ways and encourages greater inclusiveness and collaboration. Through this dialogical process, resistance to and problematization of oppression unfold, in ways that honor the dignity of our humanity and bring us into new relationships with one another.

Moreover, Freire understood that although the power to denounce and announce is born of collective struggle, it also is the outcome of politically coherent and integral human beings, who must each come to a personal decision to struggle, given that each revolutionary woman or man must live with the great joys and hardships that such a commitment entails. Hence, revolutionaries or those who are radicalized are those who, unable to persist in the oppressive values, formations, and practices of the old era, commit their passion, reason, life energy, and physical fortitude to the long historical struggle for freedom and, thus, to self-determine their own destiny as authentic human beings—extricating themselves from the limited choices presented to them by the hegemonic apparatus of schooling.

However, the transformation of material conditions cannot take place without also the transformation of consciousness, as both a personal and social phenomena. Freire considered this to be so, in that the reproduction of material conditions, whether just or unjust, is inextricably linked to the collective beliefs and actions that fuel their perpetuation. If we seek to change the material conditions that oppress the majority of the world's population, then we must recognize the ultimate purpose of an emancipatory pedagogy to be nothing less than the radicalization of consciousness—where love and political commitment inform our underlying participation in communal life and the struggle against our disaffiliation and oppression.

Radicalization

> A more critical understanding of the situation of oppression does not yet liberate the oppressed. But the revelation is a step in the right direction. Now the person who has this new understanding can engage in a political struggle for the transformation of the concrete conditions in which oppression prevails.
>
> —Paulo Freire (2002)

Despite his overarching emphasis on the role of social relationships in the formation of critical consciousness, Freire recognized that each individual must also find within themselves and in communion with others that decisive point in their lived historical process that signals their radicalization as an imperative of emancipatory life. This to say, that political consciousness and a commitment to action cannot be transferred, in a banking mode, to students or communities, no matter how oppressed. Freire (1970b) addressed this point in speaking to the question of liberation as a critical form of praxis.

> Liberation is a praxis: the action and reflection of men and women upon their world in order to transform it. Those truly committed to the cause of liberation can accept neither the mechanistic concept of consciousness as an empty vessel to be filled, nor the use of banking methods of domination (propaganda, slogans—deposits) in the name of liberation. Those truly committed to liberation must reject the banking concept in its entirety, adopting instead a concept of women and men as conscious beings, and consciousness as consciousness intent upon the world.
>
> (p. 79)

As such, the development of critical awareness requires a dialogical process whereby individuals, through their personal reflection, dialogue, solidarity, and actions over time, awaken to and evolve greater faith in their own social agency and capacity for integral formation.

To better comprehend the power and possibilities of emancipatory consciousness requires that we retain in place the dialectical qualities that underpin this process. More specifically, we radicalize and are radicalized, through relationships, labor, and struggle with one another. This, however, does not collapse the individual into the communal or the communal into the individual, in that each has a field of sovereignty and autonomy that is brought to bear, in the forging of critical consciousness. Rather than cogs in the great wheel of revolution or the historical process of evolution, we are, in fact, creators and cocreators of life—whether we participate passively through inaction and submission or bring forth critical impulses for liberation to bear upon the social and material structures that impact our existence.

An ever-present question, however, in the process of radicalization is how we make the radical option. Freire (1983) believed that the ethical man or woman "who makes a radical option" does not deny another the right to choose nor imposes that choice upon another. However, radicals do have "the duty, imposed by love, to react against the violence . . . in a situation in which the excessive power of a few leads to the dehumanization of all" (pp. 10–11). Unfortunately, it is precisely this human potential to know the world critically and to denounce injustice that is most corrupted by the lovelessness of oppression and the hostility of authoritarianism—a hostility that functions to disable the individual and collective participation and empowerment of those deemed renegades, within the existing regime.

Freire understood that if emancipatory life is indeed a journey or road to the unknown, then great courage, discipline, and commitment is required to denounce injustice and to remain ever present in the larger struggle for individual and social transformation. Rather than a perspective that objectifies the outcome of democratic struggle as some definitive endpoint or transcendent utopia, Freire understood, through his own life, that the struggle for liberation is an ongoing revolutionary and human evolutionary process, driven by a dialogical praxis, where ongoing reflection, voice, participation, action, and solidarity are key ingredients to forging culturally democratic possibilities.

Moreover, Freire considered this dialogical relationship essential to the process of radicalization and the formation of political clarity, in that critical dialogue provides a collective space in which our ambiguities and contradiction can be expressed, critiqued, and transformed, through a spirit of solidarity. As this process of radicalization implies, it requires a profound commitment to self-vigilance, particularly where ideological contradictions and historical privileges of liberal educators must be exposed; those "who proselytize about empowering minorities while refusing to divest from their class-and-whiteness privilege—a privilege that is often left unexamined and unproblematized and that is often accepted as divine right" (Macedo, 1989, p. xxx).

The radicalization of consciousness and sustained political struggle for democracy requires individuals who, through their commitment, political clarity, and love for the world, are capable of containing their arrant impulses and desires associated with unjust privilege and the internalization of oppression, if we are to move away from self-destructive behaviors or deadening forms of resistance that betray our yearning for freedom. As such, Freire believed that both reason and human compassion must inform an emancipatory educational process; but this speaks to a reason and compassion born from an integral and coherent engagement with the world, rather than prescribed forms of sentimentalism. As such, students must find opportunities to better comprehend the emotional life and to practice engaging with one another in organic and creative ways, so not to become mired in unnecessary conflict and contradiction. With this in mind, Freire counseled radical educators to practice parsimony in our communication, particularly when mean-spirited opposition threatens to derail transformation possibilities.

Nevertheless, Freire's unrelenting focus on education as a political terrain of struggle was undoubtedly fueled by his indignation over oppressive structures and exclusionary conditions enacted through hegemonic belief systems, which systematically warp how oppressed populations view our lives and surrounding conditions. Hence, any pedagogy in the interest of liberation must be geared fundamentally toward the problematization of our domestication and the transformation of the myths that conserve the oppressed-oppressor contradiction. Recognizing the difficulty of such an effort, Freire (1970b) likened it to childbirth; but implicitly linked it to the process of radicalization through his reference to the emergence of a *new being*.

> Liberation is thus a childbirth, and a painful one. The man or woman who emerges is a new person, viable only as the oppressor-oppressed contradiction is superseded by the humanization of all people. Or to put it another way, the solution of this contradiction is born of our collective labor which brings into the world this new being: no longer oppressor no longer oppressed, but human in the process of achieving freedom.

> (p. 49)

Without a consciousness of radicalization to support us, as educators who continuously must contend with repressive forces of schooling, it is impossible to support the imagination, creativity, and dreams of our students. In order to support the emancipatory dreams of others, we must believe in the possibility of our own dreams and cultivate a deeply embodied sense of how to move with an evolving consciousness of freedom through our lives. Freire (1983) also believed, drawing on the words of Karl Mannheim, that central to the process of radicalization is the need to develop "a frame of mind which can bear the burden of skepticism and which does not panic when many of the thought habits are doomed to vanish" (p. 33). What cannot be lost here is that social struggle in the midst of oppression requires that we be able to stand on our own two feet, if necessary.

Hence, the process of radicalization and, thus, critical education, must contend with both individual and social processes of transformation. In that the individual and society must be understood as dialectically indivisible in Freire's conceptualization of emancipatory life. Moreover, this dialectical relationship of human beings *and* the world is fully in concert with Freire's pedagogical vision of consciousness, as a powerful mediating political force in the classroom and out in the world.

Humility, as an indispensable quality of a pedagogy of love, is also indispensable in the process of our radicalization. Freire (1983) linked this quality to the idea that radicalized individuals are Subjects to the degree that we are able to perceive with humility both our historical and personal contradictions in an increasingly critical fashion. As such, we can never consider ourselves "the proprietors of history" but rather in a necessary communion with others "to participate creatively in the process by discerning transformations in order to aid and accelerate them" (p. 12). By so doing, as Freire illustrated repeatedly, we can become living examples of ethical beings, by engaging our conflicts and contradictions in ways that allow us to grow in awareness and apply our critical consciousness toward collective action, for the betterment of the world.

The question of faith in self and others is another tenet of Freire's pedagogy that impacts the process of radicalization;

in that faith, coupled with a deep abiding love for life, comprises a significant foundational premise for the enactment of radical hope, in our teaching and living. This sense of radical faith is closely tied to our pedagogical and political capacities to believe in those social and material conditions of liberation that we are yet unable to see in the material realm. In essence, it is the political force generated through our collective efforts that provides us the impetus to fight for social justice in schools and society. This radical faith, moreover, emerges through our critical belief in the radical possibilities of our collective reinvention.

Without such a deep sense of faith in what we might accomplish together, it is difficult to live with a critical sense of hope in the future. This understanding of radical hope, which must be anchored in concrete human possibilities, is a cornerstone of Freire's philosophy and way of life. And it is this critical hope and underlying faith in life that offers us an avenue by which we can live, dialectically, in what exists now *and what might exist* in the future to come, through our consistent love, commitment, and labor. For Freire, this radical hope develops in conjunction with the formation of critical consciousness and our radicalization, as we push against debilitating ideologies and structures that attempt to squelch our emancipatory dreams. With each transformative moment in the classroom or out in the world, our liberatory pedagogical resolve becomes stronger, as our commitment to love deepens and our political grace matures, in the process of our ongoing collective practice, as educators, activists, or community leaders for social justice.

This process of radicalization predisposes us to reevaluate constantly our lives, attitudes, behaviors, actions, decisions, and relationships in the world. It is through this dynamic process of change that conscientização develops and evolves, as we come to engage courageously the oppressive forces that impact our lives, intervening with greater confidence and strength. By confronting together the risks inherent in our radicalization, we stop surrendering our lives, our children, and our communities to the decisions of others. Inseparable here is the political commitment and responsibility required to fight for liberation, so that our destinies rest squarely in our own hands.

The Dynamic Quality of Consciousness

> Our comprehension of the future is not static but dynamic, and that we are convinced that our vocation for greatness and not mediocrity is an essential expression of the process of humanization in which we are inserted. These are the bases for nonconformity, for our refusal of destructive resignation in the face of oppression. It is not by resignation but by a capacity for indignation in the face of injustice that we are affirmed.
>
> —Paulo Freire (1998a)

To better comprehend the dynamic quality of consciousness and its critical evolution, it is useful to again turn to Freire's notion of unfinishedness. It is this epistemological dimension of his pedagogy that points to the dynamic and ever-changing quality of human live, history, and human consciousness. As conditions shift in the social and material world, so too attitudes, beliefs, and practices will shift, in accordance to our persistent critical commitment, in body, mind and heart, to create the necessary conditions for a process of decolonization to unfold. Freire (Freire and Faundez, 1989), however, noted the complexity of this process.

This process of decolonization of people's minds is slower than that physically driving the colonialist out. It is not an automatic process. The presence of the colonialist as a shadow housed within colonized people is more difficult to drive out because, when the shadow of the colonialist is driven out, the people must, as it were, fill the space it formerly occupied with their own freedom, that is, their decision-making, their participation in the rediscovery of their society.

(p. 95)

Hence, Freire reminded us to remain conscious of the flexibility and openness that emancipatory life requires of us, in order to contend with the process of decolonization and, in so doing, also embrace the unfinishedness of our existence as a hopeful aspect of humanity. This sense of hope is bolstered by the knowledge that oppression never exists as a closed or absolute system and, as such, there always exists possibilities for transformation, for those who dare push back against false illusions that masquerade as impenetrable commonsense. About this, Freire (1983) wrote,

If this historical-cultural world were a created, finished world, it would no longer be susceptible to transformation. The human being exists as such, and the world is a historical-cultural one, because the two come together as unfinished products in a permanent relationship, in which human beings transform the world and undergo the effects of their transformation.

(p. 147)

Simultaneously linked to our unfinishedness is the concept of *cultural duration*. As would be expected, Freire (1983) explained that the meaning of duration is not permanence but rather the "interplay between permanence and transformation" (p. 152) or the persistent dialectical tension between permanence and change. This dialectical interplay associated with a consciousness of liberation is important to this discussion, in that it implies an ongoing evolutionary process of human existence and, therefore, requires that our pedagogical and political efforts be well-grounded in the concrete conditions that inform their necessity.

In considering the dynamics of conscientization, Freire also noted that societies move through a variety of epochs. The shift from one epoch to another is brought about through the process of human intervention that both pushes against the themes, beliefs, and practices of the old epoch and reinvents new themes, beliefs, and practices, which move forward the process of human imagination. However, to truly participate and intervene effectively in this evolutionary process, human beings need to be able to perceive critically the conditions that shape our lives. Freire (1983) again reminded us that "a society beginning to move from one epoch to another requires the development of an especially flexible critical spirit" (p. 7). This is particularly so, given that as the contradictions between say an epoch of domination and an epoch of liberation deepen,

> the "tidal wave" becomes stronger and its climate increasingly emotional. This shock between a yesterday which is losing relevance but still seeking to survive, and a tomorrow which is gaining substance, characterizes the phase of transition as a time of announcement and a time of decision. Only, however, to the degree that choices result from a critical perception of the contradictions are they real and capable of being transformed in action.
>
> (p. 7)

This critical evolutionary understanding of history as a dynamic process, which moves from one epoch to another, is valuable to critical educators who are committed to bringing about new social and material conditions characterized by humanizing values of liberation. However, this knowledge is only useful to the extent that educators, activists, and community leaders understand that this "dynamic of transition involves the confusion of flux and reflux, advances and retreats. And those who lack the ability to perceive the mystery of the times [can] respond to each retreat with tragic hopelessness and generalized fear" (Freire, 1983, p. 9).

Accordingly, Freire called for greater individual and collective maturation in the pedagogy and politics of struggle. This necessitates a radical approach toward institutional and societal change—one that does not make emancipatory commitment, faith in the people, or hope for transformation contingent on either immediate or absolute terms. Instead, it is a politics of struggle that recognizes (1) the human push-pull evolutionary dynamics of transformation; (2) that different moments exist in the long trajectory of political struggle; and (3) the need for critical strategies and tactics rooted upon the historical conditions *and everyday life of oppressed communities.* This necessitates a pedagogical attitude anchored in reflection, self-critique, and a *disposition for change.* Of this, Freire (1998a) wrote,

> the more I acknowledge my own process and attitudes and perceive
> the reason behind these, the more I am capable of changing . . .
> it's really not possible for someone to imagine himself/herself as a
> subject in the process of becoming [critically aware] without having
> at the same time a disposition for change.
>
> (p. 44)

As new epochs approach and social conditions begin to change and radical shifts occur within individuals and out in the world, Freire believed that these can also provoke greater instances of self-awareness, as new cultural climates begin to emerge. The task at such moments is to come to perceive the old in new ways, as we begin to see ourselves and society from a new vantage point. In this way, we become aware of new possibilities that we may have not seen before. This is also the point in the process of radicalization where hopelessness begins to give way to hope as critical optimism, which according to Freire (1983),

> coincides with an increasingly critical perception of the concrete conditions of reality. Society now reveals itself as something unfinished, not as something inexorable given; it has become a challenge rather than a hopeless limitation. This new critical optimism requires a strong sense of social responsibility and of engagement in the task of transformation.
>
> (p. 13)

It is an error, however, to interpret Freire's notion of consciousness as a linear process that moves from consciousness to unconsciousness or toward some final revolutionary totality or final democratic or utopian future. Rather, it can best be understood as a spiraling epistemological process that emanates from our individual and collective engagements of self, others, and the world. As such, consciousness moves through interweaving layers of awareness, in order to emerge, time and again—according to social circumstances and human conditions—as a dynamic historical force and emancipatory expression of our humanity, which can both transform and be transformed by our organic participation in the world. It is precisely this dynamic quality of consciousness that makes the road to new possibilities for political struggle and social reinvention possible.

For Freire, conscientizaçao implies a critical awareness beyond positivist dualisms or epistemological adherences to either/or conceptualizations of life. Instead, it is born of our human capacity to discern critically the complexities and contradictions of our human condition and enter into a dynamic process of social change. This entails epistemologies of difference that engage openly the relationship between opposites in such a way that negates the very negation typical of decontextualized, reductionist, and instrumentalized conclusions of hegemonic claims. Freire's pedagogy aims toward the facilitation of a dynamic and purposeful consciousness that counters the hidden curriculum of assimilation at the core of hegemonic schooling.

Hence, adherence to a prescribed set of rigid expectations or outcomes for students is a major deterrent to the evolution of emancipatory knowledge, in that it negates all knowledge that exists outside its conscription and, thus, not only silences student voices but also curtails their right to participate actively in the process of their own learning. In Freire's articulation of the banking mode, it is this dynamic human force that readily curtailed by authoritarian schooling policies and practices. In contrast, he sought to open the field upon which the active participation of teacher *and* students becomes a vital dialectical force for the construction of knowledge and the transformation of the world. This is a participatory pedagogy that welcomes the expansiveness of being, the passion of existence, and the evolving nature of human beings to construct new knowledge, through our presence, our relationships, and the actions we undertake in our quest to know the world. Freire (1998a), moreover, considered the process of consciousness to provide us the means by which we can *experience the dynamic unity* between the contents of our teaching and the process of our knowing.

It is also through the dynamic quality of consciousness that we may come to better comprehend what Freire meant by *unity within diversity*. In that, no matter our cultural values and epistemological differences, we are all engaged in making meaning, contributing to the dynamic existence of our shared humanity, and struggling against forces that deny our humanity. Freire (1997) considered the recalcitrant structures of oppression the common enemy of all oppressed populations, contending that through the dynamic possibilities of an emancipatory consciousness, the difficulties of working across our differences could be reconciled. In *Pedagogy of the Heart*, he explained his reasoning:

> If I say unity within diversity, it is because, even while I recognize that the differences between people, groups, and ethnicities may make it more difficult to work in unity, unity is still possible. What is more: it is needed, considering that the objectives that different groups fight for coincide. Equality of and in objectives may make unity possible with the difference. The lack of unity among the reconcilable "different" helps hegemony of the antagonistic "different." The most important is the fight against the main enemy.
>
> (p. 85)

Freire hoped that a politics of unity within diversity could assist us to better struggle collectively against oppressive forces that seek to culturally homogenize schools and society, by disrupting the creative expression, cultural formation, and material well-being of racialized populations.

Oppression then may be understood as a violent force—whether physical, psychological, of political—that attempts to repress our innate human propensity to learn, grow, innovate, and create from diverse cultural centers of knowing, through which spring forth new expressions of our diverse humanity. An emancipatory consciousness emerges then from this human proclivity for curiosity and imagination, by which we dream and through our actions manifest our dreams in the materiality of everyday life. To commit to the common good and respect for the dignity of all life is the underlying measure by which emancipatory dreams are actualized, within the particular cultural contexts in which these emerge.

There is no question that what underscored Freire's pedagogy of the oppressed was an uncompromising commitment to the oppressed and an unlimited faith in the universality of our human survival—the driving force that underlies liberatory struggles no matter our cultural differences. Hence, only through ongoing dialogue and respect for the voices and participation of the oppressed and our self-determination and self-formation, can education work in the interest of culturally democratic life. This assumes a shared human kinship and solidarity that shifts unitary concerns for our cultural particularities to the dialectical realm, where emancipatory political consciousness opens the field for *unity within diversity* to unfold, as a shared human value.

In essence, the process of conscientizaçao acts as a significant transformative force between cultural differences and human universality. Here in lies the Freirian paradigmatic shift from assimilative and binary engagement with cultural differences to a dialectical paradigm, where both the particularities and universalities are essential, not only to human emancipation but to our very survival on the planet. In this light, one of the most significant features of Freire's idea of consciousness and its role in education includes a new political articulation of the relational and creative forces of consciousness, from which we cocreate a dynamic field of possibilities to be embodied in theory and practice. Here in lies the power of a problem-posing pedagogy that problematizes all that thwarts our freedom to be and struggles for the restoration of our humanity

Yet, it would be as wrong to conceive of Freire's notion of pedagogy as solely focused on the larger social structures of society, as it would be to reduce this powerful construct to merely another instrumentalized method of teaching literacy. Both views shatter the dialectical tension and transformative potential that is at the very heart of critical dialogue. Hence, Freire's philosophy of education invites us to engage politically as dialectical thinkers in the classroom and in our communities. The collective process of struggle is inextricably linked to the individual struggle that each of us is willing to undertake in our own lives. Repeatedly, Freire's writings bear witness to the unfolding and deepening of his philosophical views, in conjunction with his personal foibles, struggles, and contradictions. The notion that we are historical beings, that knowledge evolves in historicity, and that the power of our lived experiences must be cultivated as a source of knowledge and self-understanding are central to the many choices Freire made, during the evolution of his life as a theorist, a lover of life, a restless learner, a curious man, and a political comrade in the world.

The Educator and the Emergence of Consciousness

> Whereas banking education anesthetizes and inhibits creative power, problem-posing education involves a constant unveiling of reality. The former attempts to maintain the submersion of consciousness; the latter strives for the emergence of consciousness and critical intervention in reality.
>
> —Paulo Freire (1970b)

Freire beckoned revolutionary educators and leaders to embrace the labor of teaching, both as a personal and political process. In order to create the conditions for genuine student empowerment, educators had to also embrace the struggle for their own personal and collective empowerment. In this sense, Freire understood the pedagogical struggle for the transformation of material conditions had to be conceptualized in conjunction with the formation of critical awareness. And this pedagogical process could only be enacted by educators who themselves were committed to a larger project of social transformation. This political resolve was evident in Freire's life and throughout his writings, in that his pedagogy of love was founded upon an ethics and practice committed to an emancipatory vision, made possible through a growing political consciousness in the interest of freedom.

Freire understood that this entailed a radical choice that had to be made. No one could force anyone to undertake the risks and labor of a transformative commitment. It had to be a deeply sincere and radical decision that each educator had to come to within themselves. In this respect, Freire was incredibly thoughtful, open, and accepting of the difficulties and risks that such a decision meant in the life of radical educators. A true commitment to social justice had to entail a serious commitment, anchored in the knowledge of what such a choice required of us—an internal commitment to both personal integrity and a lived solidarity, in our personal, pedagogical, and political relationships.

One might say that Freire (1995) viewed his labor as an educator as a calling to a path of liberation and an emancipatory vocation, which served as an expression of his raison d'être in the world as a historical subject and political being. With this in mind, he also touched the importance of becoming clear of our own purpose so that we can take charge of our praxis:

> In my case, I am in the world because I would like to accomplish one of my tasks which is to contribute to changing the world. I discovered that very early in my childhood. I could not have come to the world in order to preserve the world as it is. I do not believe in immobility in history. I want to make some contribution to change, to transformation because it is by transforming that we make it better.
>
> (p. 19)

For those of us that see our dedication to our labor as educators similarly, this is not a commitment for the faint of heart, but rather one that demands we come to social struggle with a critical awareness that is deeply tied to a critical praxis that brings a presence of heart, mind, body, and spirit. This, of course, presupposes an empowered and developed consciousness, where the capacity for imagination, creativity, concentration, purpose, action, faith, humility, beauty, and love coalesce, in the struggle for our humanity and an evolutionary process that seeks steady erosion of ideologies, structures, and relationships that interfere with the emergence of critical consciousness.

Freire also knew, through the power of his lived history, that each person has to come to the struggle against oppression through our own conscious commitment, which means again that it cannot be coerced or imposed. Without such a deeply held commitment, major contradictions are likely to predominate, given that conflicting issues that weaken our resolve may remain hidden. And, as such, real possibilities for the development of strong social movements—that could lead us toward greater emancipatory consciousness and, hence, the necessary material transformation within institutions and society—cannot unfold.

In many ways, Freire's pedagogy and life were deeply anchored to political commitment and spiritual resolve, in that he sought to be *in communion* with students and communities whose lives were most vulnerable under capitalism. In many ways, he surrendered his life to the quest for knowledge in the interest of human liberation, recognizing that his life's work would be but one small contribution to the long historical struggle for freedom. In many of his writings, he often spoke to the question of fear and its impact, in that he recognized that fear can constrict and constrain the social agency of many well-meaning educators, obstructing their ability to fight with resolve for the transformation of educational practices, which they themselves saw as destructive to their teaching and the lives of their students.

Freire recognized that the trenchant individualism of mainstream life under capitalism, reinforced in the preparation of teachers and the structure of education, interferes with the ability of many educators to move beyond individualistic interests to invest themselves in a larger collective emancipatory project. Impaired often by conditioned fears of losing their livelihood or sense of personal independence or control, many educators persist in enacting contradictory forms of consciousness that derail the collective movement necessary to transform schools and society. As witness to his own life and that of others, Freire understood that a solid commitment to liberation does not diminish our personal sovereignty, but rather enhances personal empowerment through the political grace and maturity generated from our ongoing communal participation in social struggle (Darder, A. & Z. Yiamouyiannis, 2009). This is directly tied to the manner in which critical praxis and the solidarity it informs works to disrupt the isolation and alienation engendered by hegemonic institutions. As such, through our collective commitment to struggle with others against oppression, we open ourselves to the development and evolution of collective consciousness and the knowledge necessary to overcome the limitations of oppressive forces that limit emancipatory possibilities.

As such, it is through our genuine commitment to social struggle that we find the wherewithal from which to build our human capacity as activists—a capacity which enhances both the quantity and quality of our pedagogical and political resolve. This emergence of consciousness occurs through our individual and collective actions, in the name of justice and freedom. Accordingly, this emancipatory process can work to widen our rationality, providing us glimpses into the unlimited possibilities for reinventing our world. In contrast to hegemonic or fixed epistemologies of power that dominate schools and society, Freire advocated for an evolving political consciousness imbued with the courage to imagine new ways of learning, living, and being in the world.

Yet despite our most heartfelt commitment, Freire viewed the fight for our liberation as an arduous path that requires enormous self-vigilance and personal determination, given the powerful forces of negation at work in the world that limit and restrict our lives as subjects of history and cultural citizens. Through the subordination of the majority of the world's population, those in power have created a closed meritocratic system of capital that preserves inequalities and social exclusions. Through the advancement of positivist assumptions and exclusionary paradigms that today privilege science, technology, engineering, and mathematics, the majority of the world's population is more and more excluded from decisions that mark the destinies of our communities.

Hence, our personal struggles—particularly for those of us from working class and racialized populations—are as demanding as the larger societal struggles we wage. In many ways, this may be understood as the dialectical manifestation of the oppressed-oppressor contradiction, given the manner that structures of banking education and the culture industry constrict the intellectual and political formation of students from oppressed communities. As such, the pedagogical formation of teachers and students often echoes a resounding need for a critical dialogical process that invites us, at all levels, to reflect deeply on the ethics of our practice and the consequences of our actions with respect to questions of inequality. This also often requires from us renewed commitment to the transformation of consciousness and significant shifts in how we comprehend and respond to our world.

Through our development of critical consciousness, we, as teachers and students, can shift away from singular notions of truth, toward a plurality of awareness where simultaneous truths exist as contextual and relational phenomena—cultural truths often thwarted by dominant epistemologies that can blind us from seeing the wisdom and power that lies beyond hegemonic beliefs. Often these epistemicides exist camouflaged in commonsensical rhetoric that presents truth as fixed, obfuscating oppressive policies and practices that perpetuate human suffering. In contrast, critical consciousness opens the field of interpretation and analysis to shed light on the hidden curriculum of schooling and official transcripts of society that conserve the interests of the status quo and devalue the lives of the oppressed.

As is evident by his writings, Freire was an ardent believer that education could serve as a political vehicle for the formation of social consciousness. However, for teachers to enter effectively in such a process also requires great personal perseverance, discernment, and patience in their own pedagogical and political radicalization as agents of social change. For Freire, education constitutes an *act of love* precisely because it requires our personal investment as teachers in the lives of our students, in ways that also require our full presence as evolving human beings in the classroom. Freire (1998a) describes this "presence" as that which "can reflect upon itself, that knows itself as presence, that can intervene, can transform, can speak of what it does, but that can also take stock of, compare, evaluate, give value to, decide, break with, and dream (p. 26). To develop the power of this presence, we must address our conflicts and contradictions, if we are to be able to support our students in engaging theirs. Moreover, this "demands constant vigilance over ourselves so as to avoid being simplistic, facile, and incoherent" (p. 51). Generally, this form of self-vigilance can also help to keep us more supple of spirit and humble in our approach to the difficulties faced by our students and their families.

It can almost go without saying that a deeply humanist philosophy is at the center of Freire's (1983) articulations of pedagogy and social consciousness. In *Education for Critical Consciousness*, he summarized his perspective on this question.

> The humanist aspect is not abstract. It is concrete and rigorously scientific. This ism is not based on vision of an ideal human being, separated from the world, the portrait of an imaginary person ... It is a humanism concerned with the humanization of men and women, rejecting all forms of manipulation as the contradiction of liberation. This humanism which sees men and women in the world and in time, "mixed in" with reality, is only true humanism when it engages in action to transform the structures in which they are reified. This

humanism refuses both despair and naïve optimism, and is thus
hopefully critical. Its critical hope rests on an equally critical belief,
the belief that human beings can make and remake things, that they
can transform the world. A belief then that human beings, by making
and remaking things and transforming the world, can . . . become
more fully human.

(p. 145)

The political formation of consciousness and the pedagogical practices necessary for its formation must then encompass this humanizing ethos—an ethos that moves us away
from egoism, fatalism, arrogance, dogmatism, sectarianism,
and all forms of ideological traps that can imprison our minds
and derail the intimacy of our relationship with democracy.
As such, Freire's pedagogy of love reflects an expansive belief
in the power of social consciousness and a deep abiding faith
in the emancipatory potential of our personal and political
labor, as empowered human beings. Further, this points to a
living pedagogical process that derives meaning and purpose
from our material existence and, as such, recognizes that in
order to exist free, we must be willing to struggle together to
contend with our right to both personal autonomy and communal sovereignty, as we embrace simultaneously our joint
stewardship of our lives, communities, and the world.

Notes

1 Reference here is to a line from the poem "*Caminante No Hay Camino*"
by Spanish poet, Antonio Machado.
2 *Prise de conscience* here is understood as a raising of consciousness or
conscious realization.

4

PROBLEMATIZING DIVERSITY:
A DIALOGUE WITH
PAULO FREIRE

[T]he more radical the person is, the more fully he or she enters into reality so that, knowing it better, he or she can transform it. This individual is not afraid to confront, to listen, to see the world unveiled. This person is not afraid to meet the people or to enter into a dialogue with them. This person does not consider himself or herself the proprietor of history or of all people, or the liberator of the oppressed; but he or she does commit himself or herself, within history, to fight at their side.

—Paulo Freire (1970b)

True to his philosophy, Paulo Freire believed in dialogue and the possibilities of coming to understand others, self, and the world through interactions where participants were willing to be present and fully open to the communal process in the exchange of ideas. He was never "afraid to confront, to listen, to see the world unveiled." This last chapter with is comprised of a powerful dialogue with Paulo and our colleague and comrade, Peter Park. It is a keen example of the power and joy of Freire's pedagogical style and his sincere interest in the lives and struggles of those he met along the way. The initial focus of the dialogue looks at some of the dynamics and struggles that were happening in the early 1990s for scholars and activist of color, who were working with the critical pedagogy "movement" and within progressive institutions. As is not unusual in critical dialogue, we began our journey together one place, but the process leads us in different directions as we unveil other questions and concerns, which speak to larger ethical questions related to difference and the ethics required in our struggle for liberation.

The dialogue took place in my office at Claremont Graduate University in 1992. In many ways, the conversation was far more prophetic than I could ever have imagined that afternoon. Twenty years later, I am struck by Paulo's generosity in engaging the concerns we were raising and the deep respect and affection that he extended when responding to questions and comments that Peter and I offered. Moreover, I am also amazed that the issues we discussed twenty-three years ago remain relevant in the current political context of universities, public institutions, and communities.

Marginalization

> I do not espouse to this term marginalization. The semantic nature of the word is troubling for me.
>
> —Paulo Freire

Antonia: How can we understand better the power dynamics at work for marginalized communities within progressive educational contexts? For example, Latinos and Chicanos in this country are considered members of a culturally subordinate group and find ourselves often marginalized within the society. As a consequence, when we attempt to work politically even within contexts where the predominant rhetoric of the organization or group is considered radical, with respect to anti-racism for example, often we still find ourselves marginalized, our participation restricted, and our voices silenced.

Paulo: My first reaction is to respond to the context of the question, which causes me to have some previous considerations, so that I can enter into the contents of the issue raised by your question. My first reflection centers upon the concept of marginalization. I do not espouse to this term *marginalization*. The semantic nature of the word is troubling for me. The marginalized man or woman is the subject that finds him or herself at the margin of the society. And objectively, no one is truly on the margins of the society. No one! Everyone is within the society. The question is to know how they are positioned within. Do they exist within that society as oppressors or as oppressed; as individuals and as classes?

I continue to insist on the existence of social classes—here in the United States, as well! Then, the concept of marginalization is an ideological invention of the powerful. When those who have power define me as marginalized, inherent in the definition there exist a hidden discourse that is grounded in the very power of ideology. So, we must ask, what does it mean to have the power to conceal inequality? What does this mean? When, for example, those in power say: "If they did not wish to be marginalized, they would not be marginalized." Or, when those in power define Chicanos, Latinos, or Blacks as marginalized. It's as if they were saying that people are marginalized because that is how they want to remain. What the ruling class is saying here is that "if they would accept the rules of the game, they would not be marginalized." For me, instead of being marginalized beings, what we are, in fact, are beings that are prohibited from being. People who are denied their right to be, to exist fully. This is my first observation with respect to the concept of marginalization.

A second observation has to do exactly with the very question. What to do in a society or organization that calls itself progressive? Or what to say or do in a context that calls itself progressive? What dynamics are at play in a "post-civil-rights" context? My understanding of this is that first of all, it is necessary for those who are call marginalized—who I called oppressed, the discriminated, those that are denied the right to be and do, but instead are stimulated to do that which diminishes their being . . . those who are seeking to overturn the existing structures in the interest of liberation, the first thing that they must do is to come to know, as scientifically as possible, how the society works—no, I would say better, how the dominant classes works—and how it creates ideological traps so that we might fall into them.

Disenfranchised groups, those who are oppressed, necessarily must fight. Without fighting, nothing is possible! Liberation does not fall from the sky as a miracle or even a gift. Liberation is a political construction. It is a political invention of the oppressed. And, it is recognized as a given that those groups who are disenfranchised, oppressed, must fight for their liberation.

But the question here, related to all this, also poses a question of strategy. When it asks, what are the power dynamics at work in a progressive context? What does one do within what is an integrated, post–civil-rights society? I would pose this question by asking how do we fight today, in today's context, for the very same vision we were fighting for in the 1960s and 1970s? The objective strategies are still the same. What changes are the tactics we use, the ways in which we struggle within new historical conditions. This question must be understood in relation to tactics used by the oppressed today that are linked to a larger strategy?

Peter: I want to pick up on that thought. I agree with you that the word marginalization is not a good word in general. But we really don't have a good word to describe racially and ethnically oppressed people in this country. We sometime use minority, but as you have pointed out, at other moments, in terms of numbers, in some areas we are not minorities at all. Minority has two meanings, then. Political minority and numerical minority. In some sense we may be numerically a majority, but politically we are still a minority. But the word minority is not good either, because it has this double meaning that can confuse and obfuscate. And similarly, the word marginalization, as you've just pointed out, has this connotation, somehow, that we are not part of society.

But I don't want to get into a semantic discussion, because we know what we are talking about here, were talking about racially and ethnically oppressed people and economically oppressed people. That's what we are talking about. If I understand what you are saying, the word *post-civil rights* or *postintegration*, like *postindustrial*, I have many problems with that. Because these terms often serve as a camouflage. For example, when people say postindustrial, it makes it seem as if industrialization does not exist anymore. Or when people use post-civil rights, it implies somehow as we have won the battle of civil rights and integration, over racism. But this is not the case at all. This is much like what is occurring in other parts of Latin America, where cruel dictatorships have been replaced by friendly dictatorships. Such as in Brazil, we have Coller, in El Salvador, we have Christiani, in Nicaragua we have Chamorro, and so on. These all came to power by elections, but their politics and the power dynamics of the society are exactly the same as before. And we can say *postdictatorships,* in such instances, but the reality is that "post" is only on the surface.

Power and Knowing

> Without knowing how this society works, the economy and the mode of production of society, we cannot work on developing new tactics . . .

—Paulo Freire

Antonia: The uses of these particular terms here are employed only to highlight that in a progressive environment, there are multiple political spheres of power. You can go into one institution or group in the United States and the politics are very right-wing conservative. Then you can go into another setting and it takes on the characteristics and the rhetoric of the civil rights movement, of cultural integration or inclusion. Yet, similar inequalities of power can still exist in both. The rhetoric does not seem to reach to the actions. That is, a dichotomy exists, steeped in major contradictions. So I'm grappling with how within a so-called progressive sphere, where the actors in power consider themselves as being "post"—not that I see them in that way at all—those of us from oppressed communities often find ourselves trying to struggle with folks who talk about themselves as if they had transcended their privilege, their elitism, their racism, their sexism, and so

on. And yet, we can find ourselves struggling tre-
mendously with these people for voice and participation in decision making, for the very reasons
mentioned above. In many respects, those who
are more affluent and privileged, when they feel
they have come to see the light, believe that they
can better speak for the oppressed than those of
us who have had battle, in the flesh, to even join
the conversation! It's as if when the oppressed
are sitting in their midst and wish to speak to our
own issues, we are deemed too naïve, too emotional, too theoretically deficient, or too politically
inexperienced.

Peter: Yes, I want to address this issue. So, the struggle
has become more sophisticated in some ways
and more difficult in others. In the old days, in
the 1960s, the enemy seemed very clear, it was
very visible, it felt tangible. There was Bull Conner
in the South; there was George Wallace. There
was Pinochet in Chile. The enemy was very clear
and groups could fight with greater focus. Now,
they hide behind the façade of friendly govern-
ments or "multicultural" institutions. So, as you
say Paulo, the tactics have to change. We need
different tactics. In the 1960s, we fought in the
streets. We fought in the courts. But, we can't
do that as easily anymore, because the laws are
there on the books. The enemy seems to have
disappeared on the surface. So we must use a
different tactic. So this is a very good question,
from that point of view. In Korea, for example,
there are more political prisoners today than

before the so-called democratically elected president went into power. It's only done more surreptitiously, in this era.

Antonia: This is the case in the United States, as well. Most people are completely unaware of the number of Puerto Rican political prisoners or African-American and Native American political prisoners that remain incarcerated. A population higher today than it was 30 years ago. The struggle continues to be very real in this United States. Our youth are dropping out or being pushed out, but blamed for their condition. Unemployment of Black and Latinos is double that of the mainstream worker. So my question is also asking: How do we continue to struggle and do so effectively, when the enemy does not show its face so readily and we are more easily held responsible for material conditions of poverty, of which we have little control?

Paulo: This is why I spoke before from my knowing of how this society functions. Because without knowing how this society works, the economy and the mode of production of society, we cannot work on developing new tactics vis-à-vis the larger emancipatory strategy because, for me, again the strategy remain the same. The strategy did not change. What did the people struggling in the 1960s want? They wanted freedom. They wanted to overcome discrimination. They wanted to be. What do people want today? They still want freedom to be. It is the same political dream for self-determination. Nevertheless, the tactics must change more quickly than the strategy. The strategy is also what it means to change history. Then we must also understand and commit clearly to the strategy, for the strategy is the nesting place for our revolutionary dreams. It is for this reason that I say the strategy changes less than the tactics, which are meant to help us reach it.

Hegemony in Progressive Contexts

Progressive contexts can also be hegemonic.

—Paulo Freire

Antonia: Well Paulo, given your statement in terms of strategy, how is racist, sexist, classist power still transmitted within so-called progressive contexts—those very places that claim to be actively challenging traditional notions of power, while simultaneously reproducing the structures and dynamics? Within groups that claim to be challenging oppressive notions of power and seeking our participation? We experience these contradictions and dichotomies still at work, politically, economically, socially, irrespective of the nice words that are being said.

As I mentioned before, we especially experience this dynamic when we are working with people who consider themselves progressive, but who enter into the struggle from entitled and privileged positions. There learn the words—devoid of revolutionary praxis—and think that they should not only be free of any critique, but that they are now even more skilled than we to speak to our own issues! And those of us who have entered from a position of oppression, find that those old power relationships are still getting transmitted and reproduced, across the educational context. And so the question, again, is how do we struggle tactically to overcome this dynamic and the overwhelming tensions that interfere with our political project for democratic life?

Paulo: First of all, I think, again, we can clarify what the question means by considering the context. Progressive contexts can also be hegemonic. The question for me is not the progressive aspect of the question, although it is important. But, for me, the question is to know if the American context can truly ever be thought of as progressive. The American society is not! Then what we have here is some people who identify themselves as progressives, some intellectuals, some workers. What we have here are some departments of universities that say they are progressive.

Antonia: Well the critical pedagogy movement, for example, is supposed to embody a progressive context, at least in theory, if not practice. Maybe if we use that context as an example, it will make things more clear here.

Paulo: But the problem here is that we must recognize that the progressive critical education movement cannot do anything alone. Then one of the rules of progressive groups must be to make efforts to spread their progressivism in their relationships across different groups.

Peter: Well, yes but what Antonia is talking about is this. There are organizations devoted to critical pedagogy, let's say, but when you look at the organizational structure, the practice of that organization is not in sync with the progressive rhetoric that it espouses. This is the dichotomy and contradiction that she is talking about—where the rhetoric of equality is one thing and the practice is another. And this is also true of other educational organizations, as well. It's truly a scandal. For example, Fielding, where you were yesterday, is in many ways progressive. Not completely; but at least, they lay claim to having a progressive philosophy. But internally, there are mechanisms that are set up, unwittingly, that stand in the way of practicing progressive education. It's not because they are bad people, but the traditional structure to which they adhere interferes.

Let me give you one concrete example. Fielding has become too large. So the old relationships between faculty and students are changing. The faculty is not able to give the same level of caring and attention to students, and students cannot relate to faculty in the same personal way anymore. So, to the extent that caring relationships between student and teacher are part of a progressive agenda—because to be progressive is not just to get technical knowledge but to also to relate to others in humanizing ways—this aspect of the work is eroding. This is becoming more difficult now because there are too many students. And the increase in students was a necessity because of economic reasons. In order to survive economically, Fielding had to take more students. And because of that necessity, the structure has changed.

As structures enlarge and change, the relationships change, becoming more bureaucratic. Practicing a philosophy of caring education has become more difficult. And this gets replicated in the administration, which is also increasing in number. So, the relationships at all levels are not as good as they should be, in terms of ethnic diversity, in terms of other forms of diversity. It's just not happening because of the growth stimulated by economic necessity. I'm not trying to excuse why it's happening, but rather illustrate that our rhetoric at Fielding is not matched by our practice as progressive intellectuals.

Knowing what Happens in Society

This is the reason that I spoke before about the need for progressive people to know what happens in society . . .

—Paulo Freire

Antonia: I believe this is why we must remain grounded in the notion of praxis. The structures are constructed to meet the objectives of a particular vision or agenda of education. In the United States, particularly since Reagan, that agenda is directly tied to schools as economic engines. In the process, the humanities are taking a hit within universities. Public schools have begun to be squeezed out by conservative campaigns that push for vouchers and charter schools. In some ways, this seems a tactic among conservatives to regain control of the educational agenda. And for this reason, I don't understand how we can work toward social change and transformation in schools and society if we don't also put some close attention to reinventing the institutional structures that govern most institutions in the United States.

Paulo: This is the reason that I spoke before about the need for progressive people to know what happens in society. Now Peter gave an example of an institute whose dream is a progressive one, but that is having more and more difficulty because it is becoming larger. Then the question for us is to consider how we continue to be progressive, in spite of these structures. This is one of the things I don't believe we do well. We become bureaucratized and dogmatic very easily, when tension related to change arises.

So if, for example, we are staunch Marxists, we must continue to do what should be done, according to Lenin. Then you see, it's impossible in this historical moment to put our hands in the air and just give up. It's also impossible to be sectarian, today. To be absolutely set on doing our politics like the 1960s or 1970s will not work. It's impossible to understand history as determinism or stagnant. To conceive a democratic future, it is something that has to happen through our efforts, today. We have to change the conception of what history means, in order for us to be able to interrupt or interfere with the structures of power in institutions and society. We should try then to separate the small progressive context inside the large context, which is not progressive. The political orientation of this country, the policies of this country are *not* progressive. We are only inside of certain small groups. For this reason I say we must work to extend our progressive message across those groups that may not be progressive but are willing to dialogue with us.

Oppressor-Oppressed Contradiction

This is to say that we are radical in words, but our pedagogy is very conservative; and, at times, very reactionary.

—Peter Park

Antonia: That is exactly the struggle we face. Exactly what you are saying, here, is what so many of us experience. Because, in truth, there are these very small progressive groups, within a large nonprogressive reality that we call American society; then within those spheres of progressive people, there is still another level. And, it is here, at this level where the oppressed-oppressor contradiction seems to reproduce itself in an even more deceptive and camouflaged manner. And, it is with great frustration that many of us continue to struggle furiously with both the external and internal contradictions at work here—with leftist scholars caught up in careerism; with sectarian anti-intellectual community groups; with artists whose art poses as political; with teacher unions that refuse to grapple beyond the question of wages; or with liberal administrators who have no grounding in a politics of emancipatory struggle!

We continue, nevertheless, because we have no choice. We continue because we know we must forge some form of unity across our differences, in order to solidify our fight against domination and exploitation. But often, it is in this very place that we find ourselves further dehumanized and broken hearted; expecting to find the solace of revolutionary love and solidarity, we found instead brutal arrogance, bitter competitiveness, and egotistical pettiness. It is immensely painful at times, making it difficult for scholars of color, who are committed and ever passionate about the larger political aims of social justice, economic democracy, and freedom to be even keel in the face of betrayals and assaults from comrades whom we respected and admired. Only to find ourselves, in a new battle for our dignity, again.

Peter: Let me talk about this from a different perspective for a moment. In the 1960s, we used to say that there were three types of radicals. There is a political radical, a pedagogical radical, and a lifestyle radical. So, many can be politically radical, but not pedagogically radical. This is to say that we are radical in words, but our pedagogy is very conservative; and, at times, very reactionary. And also, many of us have not been very radical in lifestyle either. For the men, we talked about women's liberation and then we went home and oppressed women in our lives. In our language, we did that. In our intimate lives, we did that. I think something like this is still happening, within what is loosely called the critical pedagogy movement. Many of us who consider ourselves politically progressive, but still may not be pedagogically progressive. Even many of those people who talk about critical pedagogy, they are still not practicing the pedagogy. And lifestyle-wise, they may talk about it, but down deep inside there exist the residue of sexism, the residue of racism, which is then practiced in social interactions, all reproduced without knowing so.

Antonia: And, daily, these social dynamics become transmitted as acts of power that oppress and diminish our capacity to be truly free, within many of the places we work, teach, and live—even when these are shrouded in progressive slogan or radical art. This dichotomy or duplicity is wickedly entrenched in the current multicultural contexts of schools, in the critical pedagogy spaces where we hoped to find comrades, in heart and mind. The dynamics of unexamined assumptions and behaviors that perpetuate classism, racism, sexism, homophobia, and so on, can unexpectedly, or even shockingly, rear their ugly heads within our interactions with comrades or colleagues or during our participation in communities or classrooms or union meetings, as a consequence of oppressive power dynamics and dichotomies that ultimately betray our best efforts. And in these contexts, it is even more painful for the oppressed; for we expect such treatment from mainstream conservatives, but not of those we call comrades or allies.

Peter: Yes, that's right. So, this is why I say that the structure is one thing, and how we live is another. Daily, we speak the language of racism. We speak the language of sexism. We speak these ideologies in our body language and the ways in which we live and interact with others. So unless we change the way we live, from the inside out, just talking about liberatory education or progressive politics is not going to be enough.

Political Coherence

> One of the first virtues that a seriously progressive man or woman must have is . . . to expect to create in his or her body the virtue of being coherent.
>
> —Paulo Freire

Paulo: Yes. And it is because of this that I think that one of the first virtues that a seriously progressive man or woman must have is not to expect that personal or social change is going to fall from the sky. But, instead, to expect to create in his or her body the virtue of being coherent. Consistent. One of my duties, if I am a progressive man is to diminish the distance between what I say and what I do—in all dimensions. That is I cannot be a different man at home; a different man in school; and a different man in the street. I must live my politics as a coherent man, recognizing that I will have to deal with contradictions along the way, mine and those of others.

Antonia: Yes, Paulo, exactly what you are talking about is one of the greatest struggles we are contending with right now, in terms of what we might call progressive contexts of struggle. Someone will write beautifully or talk eloquently about solidarity and solidarity with the oppressed; yet, they won't even notice that in their relationship with colleagues of color, to one extent or another, they've taken a position of dominance that simply replicates the larger structures of power and ideology that we are supposedly fighting to denounce and reinvent in the first place.

And when, in the spirit of solidarity—which for me encompass a dialogical process in which to both affirm and critique one another in our work, the—contradictions are brought to their attention, they completely freak out. They freak out because they feel they are being criticized or critiqued because they are White. Or because they feel they are already giving so much to this progressive movement and therefore should be somehow above such critique. So it creates a huge clash that fractures solidarity, among those very people who could grow and learn from one another, through their mutual willingness to take on the very tasks that we are asking others to assume in their teaching and in lives. It seems that this clash occurs most when those who have enjoyed a relative sense of privilege within the progressive context are asked to tackle or struggle with their contradictions; contradictions that have an oppressive impact on the lives of working class people from culturally subordinate communities. This effort to make more horizontal, the dynamics within the workings of a diverse radical political group is very, very tricky. And, thus, it seems that there are many moments, when an effort is made to engage the issues directly and straightforward, the possibility for genuine comradeship and solidarity—born from the willingness to labor and struggle together—becomes completely derailed by the very people who preach the importance of democratic life.

Question of Ethics

Ethics has to be at the center of our pedagogy and politics.

—Paulo Freire

Paulo: This leads us to the question of ethics. Without a very strong ethical position, for me, it's impossible to change the world. Ethics, today, takes a more and more important role in history. Without ethics, we cannot seriously make a progressive movement in the United States or anywhere. Ethics has to be at the center of our pedagogy and politics. Without a very strong ethics, we are going to always be in danger of contradiction and incoherence.

Peter: Yes, I agree. Ethics is a political question that in the final analysis is always a moral question.

Positivists and political technicians would say that politics has nothing to do with morality. For example, Kissinger's politics were divorced from morality. But in the final analysis, good politics are always moral. Without morality, politics becomes an instrument of oppression.

Paulo: And the problem of coherence is a moral problem. I cannot make a speech in the morning and have an opposite practice in the afternoon. To the extent that, for example, if the weakness of people did not touch the other people, never; or if my weakness could cross the world without doing any harm to others, I could be inconsistent. But the issue is this, that the weakness of one also makes the weakness of others. Similarly, my weakness also has much to do with the formation of others. This is so, because in the last analysis, the testimony of the person is not only his or her speech; it is a communal act that affects others. If we want our speech to be of value, we should put it together as if they were just one thing at work—the speech and the action as one. But when my speech is divorced and antagonistic of my action, then the strongest part is not my speech, but rather my action.

Antonia: I am completely in agreement with you on this question, Paulo. For a person, like myself who must engage directly with issues of class daily; who must engage with issues of racism, daily; and who must engage with issues of sexism daily—all this, at times, seems like such a huge struggle. I'm 40 years old and lived in poverty, on welfare, until I was 26 years old. The majority of my life has been lived in poverty. Now, someone looks at me in the academy or on the street and they don't know the history that I carry. They don't know the reality from which I have had to struggle to be alive and here today. Yet, for me, as for all of us, that personal history is always present and is also linked to our coherence as a person; I can't cut out of me or forget the significance of my history to my political evolution, to my pedagogy. My history is always interacting with others, with the community in which I live, and the larger social reality, the political reality, which to one extent or another, still determines a great deal of my ability to be in this society.

Struggle for Voice

The people who spoke about liberating voices—including her voice— are now standing in the way and suppressing that voice.

—Peter Park

Antonia: Now, while trying to engage critically with all that, it is most frustrating to believe deeply what you are saying and to then have other people, who know little about the conditions in which, for example, I have had to survive, think that they can more accurately give better voice to the oppression that I have lived. In doing so, they inadvertently negate the hardships that I have endured to become a critically conscious woman and to find my own voice as a colonized subject of history, in these times. And how do people like me contend with those who would seek to make illegitimate our voices, even within a progressive context? How do we engage that? How do people who were once oppressed and who, by both individual and collective struggle, come to voice their own realities or reconcile themselves to this unexpected form of domination?

To, suddenly, be delegitimized by the very people who, at another moment, spoke about our oppression, about the silencing of oppressed people. Then, when those who were silenced are able to speak for themselves, suddenly a clash emerges in the progressive context. This, I tell you, is one of the most difficult dilemmas that people of color have faced within mainstream political arenas. We are accepted well as long as we speak when we are told or accept others speaking for us. To stand in the midst of our empowerment, of our social agency as political beings for ourselves, we must often wage even a trickier battle with comrades (of every color), if, critical pedagogy, as a movement, is to exist in genuine communion with the people.

Paulo: I understood that in some way you suffer a kind of ambiguity, when in having had an experience of poverty and while wanting to be loyal to the past of poverty, you have nevertheless, a present which is no longer the past. Then you think that your voice or speech today, by which you express your commitment to antiracism, antisexism, antidomination, you suppose that your speech can lose a little bit the power that it could have, if there were a total congruence between the speech and the time, for example of poverty. Is this what you mean?

Peter: Perhaps, I can speak to this. Antonia has, of course, come out of a background of poverty and silence, and now she has come out of that and in the process of doing that, she has to speak as an oppressed person—as a woman, as a Puerto Rican, in this country. And there were allies who spoke as if they were helping her to enter into this other space where there would be less oppression. But once she entered into that space, she found that the people who spoke about liberating voices—including her voice— are now standing in the way and suppressing that voice, once again. In the name of having helped her to get there, of being in alliance. But once she entered into the space where she could speak for herself, the alliance was suddenly not there anymore. Rhetorically or theoretically yes; but, in fact, in practice it is not. They do things, unconsciously perhaps, which are the continuation of the old oppressive patterns of White, male domination.

Paulo: You know how I react to this. First of all, it's normal.

Antonia: Well, yes. You can say normal, under the present ideological and material conditions of capitalism, and its repressive structures that sustain racism, sexism, and other forms of social oppression.

Dynamics of Historical Contradictions

> First of all, we should understand that history is always viewed through and inside of contradictions.
>
> —Paulo Freire

Paulo: Yes, and I would tell you something even more deeply disturbing than that. It will continue to take place in history. Today or 2000 years more, it will remain this way, unless men and women change absolutely. But being normal doesn't mean that we do not fight against it. And then this is the question of your dreams, now. That is, I think that, first of all, we should understand that history is always viewed through and inside of contradictions. This is one of the contradictions. How is it possible to suppress contradictions? Look revolutions don't have this power. The revolutions only lead to overcoming the principle contradiction of the moment; even though they thought that they could suppress all the contradictions. They thought they would suddenly be free of contradictions. But the objective contradictions continue, even after a revolution and political growth. Because in order to overcome, definitively, the contradictions, we would do what the postmodern reactionaries are saying: There is no more history. You see. No more dreams. No more utopias. Then it's possible for no more contradictions.

Paulo: But for us, convinced that history is not determined but dynamic: When you overcome a contradiction, you get another one. Another contradiction comes up that was not yet perceived, under the old ways of being. Not even imagined, maybe. But it comes up, nevertheless. The question then, for me, is to think and also to act, in order to suppress those contradictions that can be suppressed in the now. And to have conviviality, as much as possible, with the things which I cannot destroy today. For example, I also have a childhood of poverty, but today I live in a very nice house. If I was so naïve to abandon the house in which I live, in Sao Paulo to be in the periphery of the city with nothing, the first consequence is that I would lose opportunity to speak about the plight of the oppressed. Because the lack of a place to live could also make me silent. But, while I am here in this place, I have a voice. I speak to Presidents. I say what I can say. What I must say. I have, nevertheless, consciousness of the limits of my own speech; for there is nothing without limits. Nothing!

Antonia: It brings to mind that there were those who tried to keep you from speaking at one point in your life, no?

Paulo: Yes! Yes! I know that it still happens; and I too have been prevented from speaking, from time to time. Yes, I know. But I recognize this as a kind of substantive accident of history. If it were not for that possibility to liberate ourselves, why should we fight?

Antonia: Yes, Paulo I understand, what you are saying, because I often feel like I am an accident of history—for me to be where I am today, given my history of oppression, my childhood of poverty, abuse, and cruelty. It's an accident that I should be in this place and have some access, in ways that no one in my family has ever known—or the majority of people around the world, for that matter. The question, then, is: What do I do with this unexpected opportunity or privilege? How do the oppressed come to reconcile the shifts that have taken place in our lives? And what do we do with our new found voice or resources? Do we squander them or do we access and use them to support the larger struggle for our humanity. I sense that this is part of what you're getting at by your response.

Paulo: Yes, exactly. So you must see that if you leave the university, for example, you may not be stopped from speaking but you may very likely speak less. Besides, because you are here, you have much more power and opportunity to speak against injustice and oppression, than in most places where you might otherwise go. And this establishment, this institution, makes more concessions, not because this establishment loves you, but because you've got a position from which to speak. Why? Because, this establishment (true to hegemony) has to have a little consistency with its ideal of intellectual freedom and democratic speech. It's not possible for President Bush [George] in this country to say that this country is the professed educator of democracy for the world and the next day silence everyone. But where there are contradictions, there are also possibilities of constructing political pacts. Look, we must be wise. We have to take advantage precisely of the weaknesses inherent in this system of power.

Pacts and Struggle

The pact is a way of struggling, until other historical possibilities emerge for change.

—Paulo Freire

Antonia: So how do we as oppressed people become subjects of history? How do we work and theorize as full subjects on progressive agendas, with those who come from the oppressor class? From the standpoint of tactics, how do we accomplish this, given the contradictions that you so well have identified in your work and in this dialogue?

Pater: The question I believe evolves from another question: Can we dialogue with oppressive forces? Or as you say, do we make a pact with them? Because it does not seem that true dialogue is possible. Superficial conversation yes; but real dialogue no. Maybe there are other ways of doing this. These are only two choices. You can confront and challenge the power structure, making it uncomfortable by exposing contradictions. Or you can make a pact, which may endanger your integrity. Are there other ways?

Paulo: Honestly, I don't know any other way! Unless guns. But for me, the time for guns is over. At least until the next century, perhaps. Yet, even then, we would need to ask, have guns brought lasting social change? Can true liberation be born out of violence? I would say we have not accomplished this in history, even though some would say we have.

Peter: Well, let's say no guns, then. But, how about demonstrations or popular protests on the streets?

Paulo: Demonstrations, yes! But this is one of the examples, to do this there is always a need for pacts. The dominated class, the popular class, comes to the streets or strikes to create pressure, for a particular pact. This is necessary because in the first attempt to make change, the dominant class will reject a pact. Will break it, immediately! Then the dominated must use different ways, tactically speaking. They come to demonstrations, they take to the streets. They strike, and so on. One day, the dominant must accept a conversation. I call this conversation, a pact—not dialogue. I'll give a great example that took place in Brazil.

Today there is a pact that is currently in place. The automobile multinational corporations' prices are incredible. Eighty percent of the Brazilian people stopped buying cars. The car business decreased. But the multinationals don't live by just selling cars in Brazil. Instead, those who were most interested in the selling of the cars were three groups: The working class, the owners, and the government. The government of Brazil set such a high import tax that this caused the multinational corporations to sell the cars at a very high price.

But these groups decided to have a meeting last spring. Now you can bet that between the multinational and the corporation there was dialogue. But between these two elite groups and the working class, there was a pact made all in the same meeting. And what was the essence of the pact? The government reduced the tax. With the reduction of the taxes by the government, the multinational agreed to stop firing the workers. Second, they accepted not to reduce salaries; so these were two concessions which are rights, but they became coconcessions.

Absolutely, this worked for the working class because the agreement to stop firing the workers and not to reduce their salaries. From the first moment, these two conditions were absolutely necessary for the workers to say yes they would return to work. This is a pact. The essential structure of capitalism and Brazilian society was not fundamentally changed, but the workers could regroup and continue to care for their families. And this is where people make a mistake, when they say there are no more classes, no more wars between classes, no more struggle. No! The pact is part of the struggle. The pact is a way of struggling, until other historical possibilities emerge for change.

Antonia: So you are saying Paulo that we must be wise and think critically, in the manner in which to think of struggle. We must not essentialize struggle to mean only one type of action or another, since the historical conditions are also a large factor in what is possible within a society, at any point in time. So a pact are those agreements we make with the powers that be, which allow for some opportunities for working people to better their conditions for the moment, as we prepare for greater opportunities for struggle in the future. In this way, then, as you say, the pact is a legitimate tool or tactic (as you mentioned earlier), since it is a way of struggling.

Peter: Or the other way around, as well. The pact can also result of struggle.

Paulo: Yes! You are right! On one hand it is the struggle and on the other it is the result of struggle. It's the same, because it is dialectical. And look, if you're talking with the president of the national union of workers, whose power corresponds to that of a minister; who is very hard and does not make concessions beyond the limits. He stops there! He says no more will we pay for inflation! Inflation must now be paid by the rich. If you talk with him, he is a statesman. He knows how society works. This is a pact. But I think that making pacts here in the United States is difficult.

Antonia: Yes, Paulo. It is difficult in the United States to establish pacts, as you say or, at least, pacts that can truly benefit the working class and the most oppressed. The contradictions are so great here and there is a deeply suppressed history of worker solidarity, along with union bashing; to some extent, even revolutionary struggles of the 1960s seem to have not left behind a deep tradition of ongoing social struggle, beyond commercial

nostalgia. If you look at the U.S. political landscape, there are only two major parties, which
many would say are only one party, with two faces.
The evolution of serious political groups within
civil society or even a labor party, for that matter,
that could grapple over material concerns and
enter into such conversations that would produce
pacts, does not exist in the same way as in parts
of Latin America. Hence, there is a hegemonic
camouflage of people's needs, while the myth of
the rugged individual persists, to the detriment
of the most disenfranchised. In the process, the
needs of oppressed populations, the working
class, are ignored or undermined, with few public
spaces left for their voices and action to congeal
in substantive ways that would make the pact
more possible.

Peter: Yes, I want to also talk about why this is so difficult. As I said, a pact requires struggle without struggle this is not so easy. There are pacts;
and there are *pacts*. There are pacts where the
oppressor gets everything and the workers get
nothing. And then there's a pact where the
oppressed get more and the oppressor gets
less, or equal. Without struggle, that pact would
be meaningless. It would simply be another way
of telling the oppressed what they should put
up with. In order to struggle, you have to have
community. Now you're talking about a strike as
a threat and a strike in reality. That strike tactic
has become in this country less and less effective. And this is why the work of labor unions has

been less and less effective. Labor has no power now, because it has lost much of its power, as Antonia mentioned.

For this reason, they can't make the kind of pact that you're talking about. The labor unions have been making pacts on the back of the workers. We do have strikes, on occasion, but they are becoming less and less effective because in order for this tactic to work, you have to have solidarity. You have to have a community behind it. Without community, you cannot win a strike because it just fizzles out. For example, in the old days in the 1930s and 1940s, the people in the community came out and fed the workers, while they were on the strike line. There was a community that supported them. So that they knew that they could be on strike for a long time and still live. This is getting very difficult now.

Community and Identity

When we lose our ethnic identity, we lose a sense of community solidarity and cannot continue to struggle as effectively . . .

—Peter Park

Peter: A sense of community seems to be disappearing, becoming more and more fragmented. I want to bring this back to ethnic identity. This is why I think it's so important to retain racial and ethnic identity in this country, for Puerto Ricans, Asians, African-Americans, Chicanos to retain their sense of identity. When we lose our ethnic identity, we lose a sense of community solidarity and cannot continue to struggle as effectively, because it becomes an individual struggle.

Paulo: I am in complete agreement about the importance of identity. But if you don't create the connection or solidarity between the different ethnic groups, you know what happens. Each ethnic group can also become individualized, as well.

Peter: Yes, we're in agreement that the different communities must come together and find their commonalities for struggle, without losing their identity.

Antonia: You know, of course, that I agree with you both about the significance of ethnic identity. However, we must also understand that the struggle is not just about identity. We all forge a multitude of identities, as women, as men, as educators, as workers, as artist, as queer, and so on. Our ethnic identities are significant, however, given the ways in which these connect us to our histories of struggle and our efforts to survive genocide, slavery, and colonization. Nevertheless, the struggle must also, ultimately, return to the question of capitalism and material oppression; and, as you so often say, Paulo, to the struggle for our humanity and the freedom to be.

EPILOGUE
Our Struggle Continues

I believe, or rather I am convinced, that we have never needed radical positions, in the sense of the radicalness I advocate in *Pedagogy of the Oppressed*, as we need them today.

—Paulo Freire (2002)

Communities of color across the United States today are experiencing the impact of the recent economic collapse in ways that only further exacerbate many of the same social inequalities that have been at work for over a century. Mass deportations, increasing unemployment and incarceration, poor health care, severe cuts in school budgets, the vilification of public education, the silencing of parents and students, and wholesale attacks on ethnic studies programs are highly prevalent conditions in our communities, where social and material oppression are the norm. These conditions are just some of the manifestation of contemporary assaults upon working people and the persistence of racism, despite the growing diversity among the U.S. population.

As might be expected, education is at the center of many conflicts and debates, given its significant role as one of the few contested public spaces that remains within the ever-encroaching privatization scheme of neoliberalism. Hence, just as it was in the days of the civil rights movement in this country, education continues to represent a significant public arena of struggle for working class people of color in the United States—an arena where the hopes, dreams, and aspirations of our children can potentially be nurtured and supported, through an emancipatory consciousness and a pedagogy of love, as advocated by Paulo Freire.

Yet, so often the social agency of working class students of modest means and their communities are fundamentally disabled and their academic and civic needs rendered invisible by the impact of class inequalities, racialization, and other political and ideological forces that effectively obstruct democratic voice and participation—forces of cultural invasion that function to subsume the histories, languages, and futures of so many communities. Accordingly, many experience a growing sense of social alienation, as they are left to contend daily with the brutal forces of social disaffiliation, material inequality, and growing public disengagement with the needs of the most vulnerable populations.

In light of these concerns, the power of political resistance has been exemplified by educators, students, parents, and communities who, over the years, have risen up to actively resist attacks on our dignity, our expressions of culture and political voice, and our right to participate as world citizens. Freire's pedagogy of the oppressed signaled a deep philosophical moment of resistance and evolution of consciousness, in light of the political power and emancipatory possibilities it heralds. It is not a psychological mechanism nor pedagogical devise nor a mindless knee-jerk political reaction. Instead, Freire's theory of pedagogy, consciousness, and struggle is imbued with the power of love, hope, faith, responsibility, discipline, patience, courage, beauty, imagination, and perseverance, as an emancipatory practice of everyday life.

As is true in much of his writings, Freire conceived of critical consciousness not as a state of being, but as an active phenomenon born of collective struggle, rooted in the belief that as human beings participate together in reflection and dialogue about the limiting conditions—many not of our own making—that suffocate our personal and communal self-determination and aspirations, we become more conscious of the larger social, political, and economic conditions that silence our democratic participation as full subjects of history. As a consequence, our ongoing engagement with that which threatens our self-determination as individuals and communities compels us to take collective action in order to challenge and reinvent our world.

As educators, scholars, and activists, many of us continue to draw heavily upon the work of the man from Recife, as both a source of inspiration and as a conceptual guide for comprehending the limits and possibilities of resistance at this stage of history. Through Freire's understanding of political resistance and transformation, aligned with his concept of *praxis* as a regenerative process, his decolonizing vision became the harbinger of social action, critical consciousness, and political solidarity among those committed to the struggle for democratic life. Freire's emancipatory praxis then is central to an education that prepares students to become beings for themselves. But more importantly, such praxis can only be forged within the context of courageous dialogue *in community*. For it is only as we come to see the world as subjects who can act upon it—rather than as passive victims of circumstance—that we come to experience for ourselves what it truly means to be empowered human beings. And this is, precisely, what Freire meant when he wrote and spoke of empowerment as a pedagogical imperative.

There is no question that radical educators of color who have committed our lives to our emancipation, in concert with Freirian principles, continue to share this vital understanding of social agency, consciousness, empowerment, and the political commitment that this entails. As such, we embrace a commitment to the larger project of education as a means of student and community empowerment, through creating the conditions for critical literacy and political consciousness as the cornerstones of our pedagogy and our politics. This approach contrasts fundamentally with the deeply fragmented, decontextualized, and racialized meritocratic culture of high-stakes testing today, which functions, wittingly or unwittingly, to perpetuate the disempowerment and exploitation of the most vulnerable populations.

Inherent in Freire's theory of education is also an uncompromising commitment to community organizing, through critical dialogue and problem-posing strategies, in an effort to achieve a joint consciousness of what must be done to confront our own problems and to guide our collective efforts. But, above all, there is a commitment to a humanizing political vision, anchored in the recognition that without active, collective resistance within schools and society, we run the risk of not only becoming further victimized, but of also becoming more fully disempowered and silenced, even within our own communities.

Reinventing Freire's emancipatory pedagogy and politics from our unique social and cultural locations reasserts that not only is resistance to the forces that oppress our communities possible, it is absolutely essential. Freire's vision of struggle is again central to this underlying thesis. It entails a *pedagogical and political* vision that is inextricably rooted in the radical idea that one person cannot act to liberate another, but rather that through dignity and respect for one another, love for all life, purposeful and persistent dialogue, and political solidarity, we can construct together those strategies that make resistance feasible and transformation inevitable.

In *Pedagogy of the Oppressed*, Freire (1970b) rightly argued, "[a]ttempting to liberate the oppressed without their reflective participation in the act of liberation is to treat them as objects that must be saved from a burning building" (p. 65). Hence, we as educators, activists, and community leaders must continue to embrace this sentiment and, by so doing, understand resistance, not as a slogan or catch phrase, but as a powerful pedagogical process and a deeply political imperative. Through our practice in schools and communities, educators of color inspired by Freire's mandate continue to illustrate how resistance can function as an integral part of an emancipatory educational project, one that affirms our human rights, nurtures our spirits, and makes possible the fulfillment of our revolutionary dreams.

Moreover, Freire's notion of *armed love* and his dialectics of revolutionary practice continue to provide educators from oppressed communities a sound political foundation from which to launch a liberatory pedagogy of love, anchored in our ongoing commitment to our collective emancipation.

Freire (1970b) asserted, "while both humanization and dehumanization are real alternatives, only the first [is our] vocation. . . . It is thwarted by injustice, exploitation, oppression, and the violence of the oppressor; it is affirmed by the yearning of the oppressed for freedom and justice" (p. 43). In contrast, Freire articulated the conditions for the reinscribing of our humanity and by so doing, pointed to the power of education to both challenge and go beyond limit situations, in order to open the way to new futures. At a time when policy makers clamor endlessly about the importance of standardization and accountability and educational leaders peddle the latest reform gimmick or instructional flavor of the month—phonics, open-court literacy, smart boards, common core—to "save our schools," Freire's ideas continue to have salience, in our efforts to revive pedagogical debates and continue to infuse education in the United States and abroad with a liberatory vision that embraces the preciousness of life.

For more than 40 years, Paulo Freire's words have inspired radical educators of color to embrace education as a tool for empowerment, a means for disrupting poverty, an important arena of labor, a place for building solidarity, and as the most vital political tool we currently possess for countering the ignorance, bigotry, and greed of the ruling class. In the midst of groundbreaking historical changes on the technological level, the material oppression of the largest portion of the world's population persists. Nevertheless, Freire's work continues to offer us a foundation from which it is possible for us to practice education as an integral part of the struggle to decolonize ourselves—a persistent struggle essential to the future of our planetary survival.

REFERENCES

Aronowitz, S. (1998). Introduction to *Pedagogy of Freedom* by P. Freire (pp. 1–19). Lanham, MA: Rowman and Littlefield.

Beckey, C. (2000). Wicked Bodied: Toward a Critical Pedagogy of Corporeal Differences for Performance. In C. O'Farrell, D. Meadmore, E. McWilliam, & C. Symes (Eds.), *Taught Bodies* (pp. 57–80). New York: Peter Lang.

Carnoy, M. (1987). Foreword to *Pedagogy of the Heart* by P. Freire (pp. 7–19). New York: Continuum.

Darder, A. (2002). *Reinventing Paulo Freire: A Pedagogy of Love.* Boulder, CO: Westview.

Darder, A. (2011). *A Dissident Voice: Essays on Culture, Pedagogy, & Power* New York: Palgrave.

Darder, A. (2012). *Culture and Power in the Classroom* (20th Anniversary Edition). Boulder, CO: Paradigm.

Darder, A., & Torres, R. D. (2004). *After Race: Racism After Multiculturalism.* New York: New York University Press.

Darder, A. & Z. Yiamouyiannis (2009). *Political Grace and the Struggle to Decolonize Community* in J. Lavia & M.Moore (eds.) *Cross-Cultural Perspectives on Policy and Practice: Decolonizing Community Contexts.* London: Routledge.

Davis, R. (1981). Education for Awareness: A Talk with Paulo Freire. In R. Mackie (Ed.), *Literacy & Revolution* (pp. 57–69). New York: Continuum.

Facundo, B. (1984). *Freire-inspired Programs in the United States and Puerto Rico: A Critical Evaluation.* Retrieved from www.bmartin.cc/dissent/documents/Facundo/section2.html

Fanon, F. (1967). *Black Skin, White Masks*. New York: Grove Press.

Freire, A. M. A. (1995). Literacy in Brazil: The Contribution of Paulo Freire. In M. de Figueiredo-Cowen & D. Gastaldo (Eds.), *Paulo Freire at the Institute* (pp. 25–37). London, UK: Institute of Education.

Freire, A. M. A., & Macedo, D. (1998). Introduction. In A. M. A. Freire & D. Macedo (Eds.), *The Paulo Freire Reader* (pp. 1–44). New York: Continuum.

Freire, P. (1970a). *Cultural Action for Freedom*. Cambridge, MA: Harvard Educational Review.

Freire, P. (1970b). *Pedagogy of the Oppressed*. New York: Continuum.

Freire, P. (1983). *Education for Critical Consciousness*. New York: Seabury Press.

Freire, P. (1985). *The Politics of Education: Culture, Power, and Liberation*. South Hadley, MA: Bergin & Garvey.

Freire, P. (1993). *Pedagogy of the City*. New York: Continuum.

Freire. P. (1995). The Progressive Teacher. In M. de Figueiredo-Cowen & D. Gastaldo (Eds.), *Paulo Freire at the Institute* (pp. 17–24). London, UK: Institute of Education.

Freire, P. (1997). *Pedagogy of the Heart*. New York: Continuum.

Freire, P. (1998a). *Pedagogy of Freedom: Ethics, Democracy and Civic Courage*. Lanham, MD: Rowman & Littlefield Publishers.

Freire, P. (1998b). *Teachers and Cultural Workers: Letters to Those Who Dare to Teach*. Boulder, CO: Westview Press.

Freire, P. (2002). *Pedagogy of Hope: Reliving Pedagogy of the Oppressed*. New York: Continuum.

Freire, P. (2005). *Pedagogy of the Oppressed* (30th Anniversary Edition). New York: Continuum.

Freire, P., & Faundez, A. (1989). *Learning to Question: A Pedagogy of Liberation*. Trans. Tony Coates, New York: Continuum.

Freire, P., & Macedo, D. (1987). *Literacy: Reading the Word & the World*. South Hadley, MA: Bergin & Garvey Publishers.

Freire, P., & Macedo, D. (1995, fall). A Dialogue: Culture, Language, and Race. *Harvard Educational Review, 65*(3), 377–402.

Fromm, E. (1956). *The Art of Loving*. New York: Harper & Row.

Fromm, E. (1964). *The Heart of Man*. New York: Harper & Row.

Giroux, H. (1998). Teenage Sexuality, Body Politics and the Pedagogy of Display. In J. Epstein (Ed.), *Youth Culture: Identity in a Postmodern world* (pp. 24–55). Malden, MA: Wiley-Blackwell. Retrieved from www.henryagiroux.com/online_articles/teenage_sexuality.htm

Gramsci, A. (1971), *Selections of the Prison Notebooks*. New York: International Publishers.

Haraway, D. (1990). "A Manifesto for Cyborgs." In L. Nicholson (Ed.), *Feminisms/Postmodernisms* (pp. 190–233). New York: Routledge.

hooks, b. (1994). *Teaching to Transgress*. New York: Routledge.

Horton, M., & Freire, P. (1990). *We Make the Road by Walking: Conversations on Education and Social Change*. Philadelphia, PA: Temple University Press.

Lifton, R. (1990). The Genocidal Mentality. *Tikkun*, 5(3), 29–32, 97–98.

Macedo, D. (1989). Foreword to *Pedagogy of Freedom* by P. Freire (pp. xi–xxxii). Lanham, MA: Rowman and Littlefield.

Macedo, D. (1994). *Literacies of Power*. Boulder, CO: Westview.

McLaren, P. (1998) Foreword to *Pedagogy of the Body* by S. Shapiro (pp. xiii–xxvi). New York: Routledge.

McLaren, P. (2000). *Che Guevara, Paulo Freire, and the Pedagogy of Revolution*. Lanham, MA: Rowman and Littlefield.

Paraskeva, J. (2011). *Conflicts in Curriculum Theory*. New York: Palgrave MacMillan.

Seidel, G. (1964). *Martin Heideger and the Pre-socratics*. Lincoln, NE: University of Nebraska Press.

Spring, J. (1994). *Wheels in the Head: Educational Philosophies of Authority, Freedom, and Culture from Socrates to Paulo Freire*. New York: McGraw-Hill.

INDEX

alienation 6, 25, 27, 39, 51, 58, 77, 94,
    128, 167
anger 52, 53, 58, 73,
armed love, notion of 48, 170–1
authoritarianism 11, 13, 23, 28, 76,
    99, 102, 111
authority, freedom and 20, 21–2,
    32, 60,

banking education xi, 10, 18, 31–2,
    55, 59, 60, 67, 94, 96, 100, 110, 121,
    124, 129
behaviorist model 72

capitalism 1, 3, 23–32, 38, 50, 59,
    61–3, 69, 99, 127, 155, 161, 165
Christianity paradigm 72
civil rights movement 32, 33, 167
classrooms: cultural differences
    in 58–9; emancipatory 50, 56;
    indispensability of the body and
    70; issue of authority in 21–2;
    stimulating democracy in 22–3;
    student resistance in 101–9
collective consciousness 50, 66, 128
colonization x, 3, 9, 30, 33, 36, 61, 165
communities of color 9–10, 33, 166
community and identity 164–5

conscientizaçao concept:
    consciousness and 116–31; dialogue
    and 91–101; elements of 82–8;
    indispensability of resistance 101–9;
    introduction to 80–2; key notions
    84–5; probelmatization and 88–91;
    radicalization and 109–16; see also
    social consciousness
consciousness: dynamic quality of
    116–24; emergence of 124–31;
    political formation of 131;
    radicalization of 112
consumerism 23, 25, 61
contradictions, historical 156–9
critical awareness 82, 84, 121, 125
critical consciousness: as an active
    phenomenon 168; cultural
    context and 36–9; development
    of 129; evolution of 6, 7, 32;
    humanizing education and 64;
    indispensability of resistance and
    105; indispensability of the body
    and 79; integration and adaptation
    and 104–5; learning and 87–8; love
    as political force and 49–55
critical dialogue see dialogue
critical literacy 103, 169
critical pedagogy movement 142, 148

critical transitive consciousness 83
critical understanding of history
    118–19
cultural differences 58–9
cultural duration concept 117–18
curriculum: ideology of the market
    and 60; multicultural 32, 35; of
    schooling 129; standardization of
    10, 11, 62; of technology 29

decolonization 97, 116, 117,
decolonizing approach 101, 103
decolonizing forms of knowledge
    58, 60
deficit notions 33, 34, 35, 67, 73, 94,
    98, 100
dehumanization 36, 41, 42, 111, 171
democratic participation 89, 98, 168
demonstrations as way to protest 160
dialectical relationship 19–23, 81,
    86, 114
dialectical tensions 15, 84, 86
dialogue: conscientization and
    91–101; humanizing education
    and 65; with Paulo Freire 132–65;
    pedagogy of love and 57;
    radicalization process and 112;
    relational understanding of 18–19;
    between teachers and students
    21–2
disenfranchised communities 24, 44,
    101, 163
domestication 13, 26–8, 69–70, 71,
    94–96, 113
dominant culture 4, 8, 15, 94

economic inequalities 31, 33, 59
education: as an act of love 130;
    assumptions of neutrality in 8;
    "banking" system of 10, 18, 32,
    55; humanizing process 6, 63–6;
    indispensability of resistance
    and 107–8; multicultural 32–6;
    as a political act 7–14; social
    consciousness and 129–30

educational practices 13, 26, 62,
    63, 127
Education for Critical Consciousness
    (Freire) 82, 130
educators of color 34, 35, 169, 170
elitism 38, 60, 138
emancipatory classroom 50, 56
emancipatory consciousness 81, 83,
    100, 122–3
emancipatory knowledge 18, 19, 69, 121
emancipatory pedagogy 6, 65, 98, 102
emancipatory political vision 10,
    63, 96
emancipatory process 16, 55, 128
epistemicides 16, 72. 96, 129
epistemologies 4, 8, 15, 18, 35, 36, 51,
    60, 67, 74, 78, 85, 87, 96, 100, 105,
    116, 120–22, 128, 129
epistemological curiosity 51, 81, 86,
    87
equality and fair treatment 31, 61
ethics, 55, 59, 125, 129, 133, 151–3
ethnic identity 164–5
evolutionary process 81, 103, 118, 126

faith in self and others 114–15
fetishization process 25, 26
freedom, authority and 21–2
Freire, Paulo: beliefs of 65–6;
    educational philosophy of 124;
    humanizing qualities of 64; on
    oppression 2, 3; pedagogy of love
    and 52; revolutionary vision of 45;
    on violence 42
Freire's interview: awareness about
    society 144–6; community
    and identity 164–5; historical
    contradictions 156–9; introduction
    to 132–3; marginalization 133–8;
    oppressor/oppressed contradiction
    146–9; pact and struggle 159–64;
    political coherence 149–51; power
    and knowing 138–41; progressive
    contexts 141–4; question of ethics
    151–3; struggle for voice 153–5

high-stakes testing 11, 31, 35, 62, 169
historical contradictions, dynamics of 156–9
history, critical understanding of 14–19
humanization 6, 29, 39, 41, 42, 96, 113, 116, 130, 171
humanizing education 63–6

incarcerations 33, 101, 166
indispensability of resistance 101–9
indispensability of the body 66–79
inequalities: capitalism and 23, 24; class 24; economic 31, 33, 59; liberation and 128; neoliberal policies and 36; oppression and 37; of power 138; wealth 62
integration and adaptation 104–5
intolerance, oppression and 56–7
isolation and disconnection 57, 58, 128

knowledge: as historical process 14–19; standardization of 35
knowledge construction: indispensability of the body and 66, 68; pedagogy of love and 51, 57; teachers' responsibility for 21; values and beliefs and 20

labor unions 163, 164
Latinos and Chicanos 134, 135
LBGTQ youth 75
learning: critical aim of 44; critical consciousness and 87–8; dialogical reciprocity in 93–4; indispensability of the body and 68, 69, 73; pedagogy of love and 52–3; technology trend and 29
liberation: betrayal of multiculturalism and 32–6; cultural context and 36–9; dialectical relationship 19–23; education as a political act and 7–14; inequalities and 128; introduction to 1–7; knowledge as historical process and 14–19;

oppression and 136; personal empowerment and 127–8; radicalization and 110; schooling and capitalism and 23–32; unfinishedness significance and 39–45; violence and 160
lifestyle radical 147, 148
limit-situations 17, 19, 40, 90, 108, 171
love: as a dialectical force 50; humanizing education and 63–6; humility and 114; indispensability of the body and 66–79; as a political force 49–55; solidarity and difference and 55–63

marginalization 35, 104, 133–8
mass production 27, 28, 69
material conditions 70, 86, 100, 119, 125
materiality of human existence 68, 71
morality 44, 152; moral stance 5; moral potential 9; moral leadership 39, 65; moralistic agents 75; moral questions 79, 151
multiculturalism: betrayal of 32–6; neoliberal 61

neoliberalism 1, 24, 27, 28, 29, 41, 46, 167
neoliberal multiculturalism 35, 61, neoliberal policies 28, 33, 36
numerical minority 137

oppression/oppressed communities: anger and 52, 53; capitalism and 23, 30, 59–60; commitment against 126–7; communities of color and 9–10; dehumanizing fatalism and 100–1; delving into personal 106; emancipatory consciousness and 122–3; Freire's views on 2, 3; increased capacity for choice and 104; inequalities and 37; intolerance and 56–7; liberation and 136;

marginalization and 134; resistance and 14; struggle for voice and 153–5; uncovering history of 16; violence of 3, 41, 106
oppressor/oppressed contradiction 4, 113, 129, 146–9

pact and struggle 159–64
pedagogical radical 147, 148
Pedagogy of Freedom (Freire) 82
pedagogy of love *see* love
Pedagogy of the City (Freire) 21
Pedagogy of the Heart (Freire) 74
Pedagogy of the Oppressed (Freire) 1
personal empowerment 54, 127
physical expressions 67, 75
political coherence 149–51
political consciousness 5, 110, 123, 125, 169
political economy: capitalism and 30, 31; classroom knowledge and 22, 23
political formation of students 11, 13, 129, 131
political minority 137
political prisoners 139, 140
political radical 147, 148
political resistance 14, 167, 168
populations of color *see* communities of color
post-civil-rights society 135, 136, 137
power, inequalities of 138–41
prescribed, notion of 10, 12, 44, 54, 81, 90, 98, 99, 100, 103, 104, 112, 121
problematization 88–91
problem-posing pedagogy 32, 100, 103
process of fetishization 25, 26
progressive contexts: ethics and 154; hegemony in 141–4; of struggle 150, 151
public schooling 13, 24, 144–5

racialized communities 23, 26, 37, 73
racialization 30, 167

racism xii, xiv, 2, 3, 38, 56, 68, 79, 101, 134, 137, 138, 148, 149, 152, 155, 167,
radicalization 109–16, 120
relationships of solidarity 50–1
resistance: dialectical relationship and 19–20; oppression and 14
revolutionary love 62–3, 147

schooling: capitalism and 23–32; curriculum of 129; hegemonic practices of 51, 58, 59, 69, 89; political economy and 31–2
schools: class privilege perpetuated by 97; notions of neutrality within 96–7; as political sites 8–9; technology trend in 29
semi-transitive consciousness 83
sensuality and sexuality 74, 75
social consciousness 79, 81, 82, 130, 131
social control 44, 72
social justice 48, 97, 115, 147
social transformation 5, 80, 83, 125, 145
solidarity relationships 50–1
standardized curricula 10, 11
structural inequalities 24, 79
students: dialogue between teachers and 21–2; educational conditions of 23; indispensability of resistance and 101–9; indispensability of the body and 67, 73, 76, 78–9; pedagogy of love and 53–5; political formation of 11, 13, 129, 131; problematization and 88–91
students of color 20, 31, 52

teacher preparation programs 34, 71
teachers: authority issues 21–2; capitalism and 29–30; emergence of consciousness and 124–31; evaluation issues 12–13; indispensability of resistance and 108–9; indispensability of the body and 77–8; pedagogy of love and

53–5; responsibility of 32; reward and punishment system for 11–12; students' political formation and 11, 13

Teachers as Cultural Workers (Freire) 43

teacher-student relationship 57, 90

teaching: dialogical reciprocity in 93–4; indispensability of the body and 68, 69, 73; learning from students through 106–7; loving the process of 55; pedagogy of love and 52–3; political understanding of 13–14

technology, capitalism and 29

"training" programs 98

transitive consciousness 83

unemployment and underemployment 27, 31, 101, 166

unfinishedness, significance of 39–45, 116, 117

unity within diversity 59, 122, 123

violence: Freire's views on 42; liberation and 160; of oppression 3, 41, 106

voice, 4, 6, 16, 53, 67, 71, 89, 98, 100, 102, 111, 121, 134, 139, 163, 167; struggle for 153–5, 157, 158

wealth inequality *see* inequalities

workforce: alienation of 25, 27; capitalism and 23, 24

working class students *see* students